SOUTH SIDE HIGH SCHOOL

THE FIRST
SEVENTY-FIVE YEARS

BY G. STANLEY HOOD

South Side High School Alumni Association, Inc.

Fort Wayne, Indiana

1996

SOUTH SIDE HIGH SCHOOL
THE FIRST SEVENTY-FIVE YEARS

Printed in the United States of America by
Lincoln Printing Corp., Fort Wayne, Indiana 46895-5166

Library of Congress Catalog Card Number: 96-092736

Cataloging-in-Publication Data

Hood, G. Stanley, 1938 -
    South Side High School: the first seventy-five years (1922-1997) / by G. Stanley Hood. -- Fort Wayne, Ind. : South Side High School Alumni Association, 1996.
    152 p : ill. ; 29 cm.
    Includes Notes and index.
    Contents: Chapter one (1922-29), The early years; The arrival of R. Nelson Snider; We become "The Archers" -- Chapter two (1930-39), The depression; State champs; Growing pains, we add a second floor -- Chapter three (1940-49), Archer Green goes to war; Twenty-five candles on the cake -- Chapter four (1950-59), I like Ike and Elvis too; State champs again; More construction, but still no auditorium -- Chapter five (1960-69), Time does not stand still; Jack Weicker takes command; Dress codes and Vietnam -- Chapter six (1970-79), Finally an auditorium; The golden anniversary; Presidents don't resign, do they? -- Chapter seven (1980-89), Girls' state track champions, four times; Athens in ruins? The school that saved itself -- Chapter eight (1990-97), Jennifer Manth and South Side pride; Renovation and the new campus; Diamond jubilee.

ISBN 0-965-51440-4   977.274

CONTENTS

PREFACE AND
ACKNOWLEDGEMENTS

Seventy-five years is a lot of history. We do not pretend to have covered every aspect of it. This is intended to be a general history of the development of South Side High School with some attempt to connect intra-school events with events that were happening contemporaneously in the city, state, nation or world. No attempt has been made in this chronicle to establish lists of valedictorians, salutatorians, four-year honor roll members, National Honor Society members, or class officers. These are separate and distinct endeavors, and it is hoped that such listings will be produced by the administration of South Side High School during this seventy-fifth anniversary year. Detailed sketches of such things as club activities, present and former faculty members, and other aspects of student life at South Side High School would obviously lend themselves to creating separate books on each. Many of the people and events that have been left out of this history are just as important to the development of South Side High School as those who have been included. Obviously, the production of a work such as this involves some subjectivity on the part of the author, and we are inevitably left with the result that "history becomes what those who write it say it was." Hopefully this endeavor will be viewed as a satisfactory attempt to chronicle the general history and development of South Side High School, one of the nation's truly outstanding educational institutions.

The assistance, participation and inspiration of many people are necessary to accomplish a project such as this. I would like to recognize some of those individuals. My sincere thanks and appreciation go to Steve Fortreide and Janet Hartzell of the Allen County Public Library. Prominent local historians Michael Hawfield and George Mather were especially helpful with their encouragement and advice on certain technical matters. Jennifer Manth and Beverly Wyss of South Side High School provided me with free access to the building at all times, and Kathy Kerbel and Dr. Anne Spann of the media center at South Side were especially helpful to me during my research of old volumes of the *South Side Times*. Likewise, Kathryn Zaegel of the South Side Alumni office rendered invaluable assistance in providing certain materials. Special appreciation is extended to George Robert Davis, "Mr. South Side," for his special knowledge and insight into the history and traditions of the school and for lending me on numerous occasions his personal collection of *Totems*. Likewise, I want to extend a special thank you to the people who allowed me to interview them, and in particular, two of my favorite teachers from my days at South Side, Jack Weicker and Mary Graham. Miss Graham, I hope that not too many of my sentences ended with prepositions.

Finally, I want to recognize three people without whose assistance I could never have completed this project. These three individuals are Jim Croxton of Lincoln Printing, Tammy Wells, my legal assistant, and my wife, Ruth. Jim Croxton graduated from South Side High School High School with the class of 1952. He is responsible for the creative and imaginative selection and layout of photographs which appear in the book. Jim's knowledge of South Side High School and its traditions, coupled with his excellent knowledge of the printing business and his high degree of professionalism and infinite patience made him the ideal person to coordinate this project. Tammy Wells has been a part of this project since the beginning and has never ceased to be her usual cheerful and dependable self through a never-ending series of drafts and redrafts. To my wife, Ruth, goes my profound and sincere thanks and appreciation for putting up with nearly two years of lost weekends, a neglected social calendar and even the "occasional" bad mood.

PREFACE AND ACKNOWLEDGEMENTS

I wish to reserve special thanks and acknowledgement to the South Side High School Alumni Association for their financial underwriting of this project. Without their generosity, this book could never have been published.

It is our hope that this book will not only bring back a few memories but will impart some insight into what South Side High School has been, and more importantly, what it has become—an institution in which we can derive a high degree of pride from past accomplishments and gain well-founded optimism for the future. Our greatest hope is that this magnificent educational institution will continue to pursue its noble mission and when the 100 year history of South Side High School is written, that this book and the information contained herein will provide some assistance.

October, 1996   G. Stanley Hood

INTRODUCTION

I left the media center, which for more than seven decades was the location of the gymnasium. As I exited through the familiar north doors which now serve as the main entrance to South Side High School, the rain was gently falling on the asphalt of the parking lot where the football stadium once stood.

There were few cars in the parking lot for this was June 6, 1996, the final day of the school year. As I walked toward my car, I saw a solitary figure loading books and other items into a Buick sedan. As I drew near, I recognized this person as George Robert Davis, a member of the South Side graduating class of 1952. This was the same George Davis who for nearly 40 years taught chemistry at South Side. Walking toward George, I noticed the rain clouds of the early June day had parted bringing forth the illumination of brighter skies.

As the first rays of the newly-liberated sun appeared, I looked over my shoulder at the remodeled building with ivy-covered walls which had experienced 75 years of educating and inspiring thousands of students. The magnificence of the architecture and the new rays of sunshine gave rise to the promise of many years of future activity in the education of the young minds of our community. The eyes of the man I was approaching looked wistfully over my shoulder, and I knew that he too was looking at the building now basking in the splendor of the late afternoon sun. Unlike the building, he did not share in the promise of future years as an educator for this was the final day on the job for George Robert Davis. As I put my arm around him and wished him well, his eyes were moist. His speech came haltingly as he said, "If I were doing it all over again, I wouldn't do one thing differently. I will really miss teaching. All I ever wanted to do was teach in this building. I love this building." I replied, "The building loves you George and so do the thousands of students whose educational experiences at South Side were more meaningful because of your influence."

As the Buick sedan disappeared from view heading north on Calhoun Street, an era came to an end at South Side High School. The departure of George Robert Davis into retirement recalled memories of a similar day in 1964 when his father, Ora Davis, ended his 40 years of service as a member of the South Side faculty. When school reopened at South Side in the late summer of 1996, for the first time since 1923, there was not a Davis on the faculty.

South Side Alma Mater

Hail to thee, O South Side High School,
Faithful may we be;
Our beloved Alma Mater,
We sing our praises to thee.
May we always well remember
All thy gifts to us so free;
And pay homage to thy memory,
Hail, South Side High School, to thee.

Words by Jack Wainwright

CHAPTER ONE
1922 TO 1929
A. The Early Years

On September 11, 1922, the guns of World War I had been silent for less than four years. The president of the United States was Warren G. Harding, a former United States Senator from Ohio. President Harding would die in office, and would be succeeded by Calvin Coolidge. The city of Fort Wayne, Indiana, had a population of 86,549. On September 11, 1922, South Side High School opened its doors to students for the first time. The idea of a second high school in the city of Fort Wayne became a reality in 1920 when Fort Wayne High School (later known as Central High School) became over-crowded. As a site for the new high school, the school board chose a tract of land on South Calhoun Street close to the city limits. The land on which the school was constructed had been used for gardens by the residents. The land on which the football stadium was constructed was rather flat. This site had previously been occupied by the Kaylor Brickyard. At the present north entrance of South Side High School where Darrow Avenue once ran, there used to be a creek called Shawnee Creek or Shawnee Run. A bridge spanned the creek close to the present north entrance to the school. After Calhoun Street was paved, the creek gradually filled up with rubbish and trash.[1]

The architectural style of the South Side High School building is Grecian Ionic. The material used in the construction of the building was yellow brick and Indiana limestone. There were 200 tons of radio brick included in the old powerhouse smokestack which was 150 feet high. To level the ground, 20,000 cubic yards of dirt were removed. Seven thousand cubic yards of concrete and 42,000 square yards of plastering were used. Fifty-two thousand five hundred feet of metal trim (nearly ten miles) were used in the construction. The linoleum which is one-fourth of an inch thick totaled 12,000 square yards, and the school building weigh-ed 30,000 tons. There were 838 windows.[2] The cost of the initial construction of South Side High School was 881,672 dollars for the building and 53,619 dollars for the stadium. Construction was started on September 1, 1921, and even though the build-ing was not totally finished, it opened to students on September 11, 1922.[3]

The Football Stadium – 1924 Totem

When South Side High School opened, it was said to have been the largest one-story school in the country. The building itself covered three acres and the normal capacity was 1,500 students. The football stadium could accommodate 3,200 people, and the gymnasium could hold a crowd of 2,500.[4] Actually, it was somewhat of a misnomer to refer to the new South Side facility as a one-story school. There were a limited number of classrooms and offices on a second floor. There were no stairways in the building; inclines took their place. Rooms 174, 176 and 178 located above the botany classroom along Gumpper Avenue (now Oakdale) were reached by the so-called south incline. This incline was later closed at the time of the 1938 remodeling which added a full second story and stairways. Rooms 138, 140, 142, 144, and 145 located on the east side of the building were reached by the middle incline. The teachers' rest room, office, and library were also reached by the middle incline, although they were located above the Calhoun Street entrance. The cafeteria located above the north entrance was reached by the north incline.[5]

When South Side High School opened its doors, classes were held primarily in the south part of the building because the north section, particularly in the area of the gymnasium, had not as yet been completed. To further complicate matters, the approximate 800 high school students shared the building with 510 grade school students. The South Side Grade School continued to be a part of the facility until the autumn of 1925 when Harrison Hill School opened. The principal of South Side Grade School was Charles A. Agnew who became the first principal of Harrison Hill. The grade school was located in the south part of the building.[6] Mr. Herbert Voorhees, long-time South Side chemistry teacher, commented on the early weeks of classes as follows: "Since there was no door to my room, I shouted chemical symbols above the accompaniment of a concrete mixer in the place where the gymnasium now is."[7]

To relieve the cramped circumstances, portable buildings were placed on South Field located on the south side of Gumpper Avenue (now Oakdale) across the street from the main building. These portable buildings were used primarily by the students of the South Side Grade School, and there was little or no ventilation. Robert Parrish, Fort Wayne attorney, president of the South Side class of 1934, and former student of the South Side Grade School remembers when the weather was hot, the students would be sent home because of these ventilation problems.[8]

When South Side High School first opened, desks and other furnishings had not been delivered to the classrooms. As a result, students frequently had to sit on nail kegs. Because construction was not completed, half-day sessions were held for several weeks until October 30, 1922, when the first full-day session took place.[9]

South Side High School's first principal was Robert C. Harris. Mr. Harris earned his Bachelors Degree in mathematics at Indiana University, and his Master of Arts Degree in education from the University of Chicago. He

Robert C. Harris

taught in several rural Indiana communities and during the 1913-14 school year was principal of Central High School in San Juan, Puerto Rico. Following this principalship, he taught math and physics at Manual Training High School in Indianapolis for three years. In 1917, Mr. Harris joined the faculty of Fort Wayne High School where he taught physics for five years. Mr. Harris served as principal of South Side High School for four years. For the next twenty years, he was principal at James H. Smart School retiring in 1946. He had many outside interests. He became an expert on Johnny Appleseed. In addition, he was the writer of two math textbooks. Among his talents, Mr. Harris was an inventor. He developed an electrical pulse generator in 1937 which was transformed in 1942 into a trigger device used on bazookas and other rocket launcher guns. A magnetic firing key, a relay activator, an automatic contact maker, a vision coin counter, an alphabetizer, model railroad devices, and a range finder were among the other cre-

Martha M. Pittenger

ations of Mr. Harris. On May 1, 1957, it was announced that Mr. Harris had been named Teacher of the Nation for that year by the National Council of the Senior League. He received the "Apple of Gold" award at the Teachers' Remembrance Day Banquet in Los Angeles on June 2, 1957.[10]

South Side High School was blessed with an excellent original faculty consisting of thirty-seven teachers. Many of the original faculty members transferred to South Side from Fort Wayne High School (Central High School). Included among these was Martha Pittenger who became Dean of Girls. Miss Pittenger was to hold that position until 1950. George Robert Davis, South Side graduate and long-time faculty member, recalls that Martha Pittenger and Robert Harris used the same desk. It was a two-person desk with Mr. Harris sitting on one side and Miss Pittenger sitting on the other side.[11] Sixteen of the original faculty members were still on the staff in 1947 when South Side High School celebrated its twenty-fifth anniversary.

Late in September of 1922, the students of South Side High School held a pep session in the partially completed gymnasium. At this time, green and white were unanimously selected as the school colors. A song written by a student, Paul T. Hahn, entitled, "Our School" sometimes referred to as "To The School That Has No Equal" was adopted as the school song.[12] The first issue of the school newspaper, the *South Side Times*, a four-page version, appeared on October 6, 1922. Ruth Wagner was the first editor-in-chief. During the second semester of the 1922-23 school year, Willis Carto was editor-in-chief.[13]

For the next two decades, the *South Side Times* consistently won top honors from several scholastic press associations including "Best High School Paper in Indiana," "Best High School Paper East of the Mississippi," and "Best High School Paper in the United States." The publication of the school paper created a debate as to whether "South Side" was to be one word or two words. Following the publication of three issues of the *Times* in which "Southside" was designated as one word, Principal Robert Harris decreed that henceforth "South Side" would be two words. Consequently, the fourth issue of the *South Side Times* published on November 3, 1922, was the first issue in which the banner carried "South Side" as two words.[14] Late in 1922 during the first year of its existence, the *Times* entered a contest at Madison, Wisconsin sponsored by the Central Interscholastic Press Association (CIPA). The *Times* was adjudged to be the best high school paper in the State of Indiana. At the same time, a national contest was held.

Our School

1923 Totem

A rather embarrassing incident occurred when the *Times* was mistakenly thought to be a junior high school newspaper and was awarded first place for junior high school newspapers. Later, when the judges discovered it was a high school paper, they refused to change the award. Consequently, the *Times* had to wait one more year before being adjudged the best high school paper in the nation.[15]

The faculty advisor of the *Times* for 37 years was Rowena Harvey. She attended Shortridge High

Rowena Harvey

School in Indianapolis and was editor-in-chief of the Wednesday *Echo*. At that time, Shortridge published a four-column newspaper every day of the school week and had a different staff for each day. Following her graduation from high school, Miss Harvey attended Indianapolis Normal School, and at the same time was a free-lance writer for the *Indianapolis*

4 - "The Best in Indiana" was the title won by the *Times* when just six weeks old. That title brought pleasure but - -

5 - The thrill of a lifetime came when the paper, a little over a year old, was proclaimed the best in the United States by the C.I.P.A. delegates assembled from all corners of the United States.

1922 FOOTBALL SQUAD – UNDEFEATED
Back Row (left to right): W. Gilbert (Coach), J. Haynor, A. Fromouth, E. Aldrich, P. Oliver.
Middle Row: P. Knapp, L. Emerson, D. Parker, L. Ridgway, R. Hanna.
Front Row: L. Wilkens, E. Rahe, R. Jurgensen, L. Norris, D. Sprang, R. Plasterer, P. Williams.

News and the *Indianapolis Times*. She received her AB Degree with the highest distinction in English at Indiana University in 1921. At Indiana University, she became the second woman in history to be editor-in-chief of the *Indiana Daily Student*. When North Side High School opened in 1927, she was also made a teacher of journalism at that school and was in charge of the press for the Fort Wayne Public Schools. Consequently, for several years she was faculty advisor for both the *South Side Times* and the *Northerner* (the school paper at North Side).[16]

Since the football stadium was not completed when South Side High School opened in September of 1922, it was originally thought that the school would not field a football team during the first year. Due to the presence of Ward O. Gilbert and the enthusiasm of the students, it was decided that a six-game schedule would be played and consequently South Side would have a football team in the fall of 1922. Mr. Gilbert organized the first team which practiced both at Weisser Park and at the almost completed South Side gymnasium. On October 12, 1922, South Side played its first football game and defeated Auburn 26-0. The honor of scoring the first two touchdowns in South Side history went to Edwin Aldrich. The other two touchdowns were scored by Alan "Red" Fromuth and John Haynor, each of whom made a 40-yard run. South Side went undefeated in its first football season winning all six scheduled games, including a season ending 9-6 victory over arch rival Central. Alan "Red" Fromuth booted a 15-yard drop kick field goal to win the game. The 1922 football team scored a total of 139 points while holding the opponents to just 18 points. Fromuth was the leading scorer with 67 points and was also captain of the team. Members of the first South Side football team in 1922 were Louis Ridgway, Park Williams, John Haynor, Louis Norris, Dan Sprang, Leslie Emerson, Donald Parker, Robert Jurgenson, Edward Rahe, Paul Oliver, Edwin Aldrich, Paul Knapp, Robert Hanna and Louis Wilkens.[17]

An unfortunate postscript to the 1922 football season occurred in January of 1923 when Arthur Trester of the State Athletic Association investigated the eligibility of Dan Sprang, one of the South Side players. Confusion caused by the transfer of a great number of pupils from Central to South Side High School during the first year resulted in Sprang being declared eligible when he was really ineligible due to the four-year rule. Consequently, the three games in which Sprang participated, which included the

1922-23 BASKETBALL TEAM – SECTIONAL CHAMPIONS
Left to right: Top Row–R. Plasterer, L. Norris, A. Fromuth, W. O. Gilbert.
Bottom Row– G. Wyss, E. Englehart, P. Williams, D. Parker, L. Wilkens.

Central game, were forfeited. This episode marked the first chapter in a long-running battle between South Side High School, its principal Robert Harris, and the Indiana State Athletic Association. As a result of this feud, the Indiana High School Athletic Association later suspended South Side for a period of one year.[18]

Ward Gilbert, who was South Side High School's first football and basketball coach as well as first athletic director, taught at South Side from the opening of the school in 1922 until his retirement 37 years later. Mr. Gilbert obtained his Bachelors Degree from Indiana University, and as an undergraduate won letters in every major sport except football even though he played football. He excelled in baseball and basketball. He was a member of the IU baseball team that visited Japan in 1921 and pitched the only two games won by IU on the Japanese tour. While playing basketball in the Big Ten Conference, he had the distinction of being the shortest center in the league. During the 1916-17 season, he won the state basketball championship of Florida while coaching at Winterhaven High School.[19]

On November 25, 1922, South Side's first basketball team, coached by Ward O. Gilbert, and referred to as the "Caging Squad" played its first game and lost to Auburn by a score of 23-12. South Side made only one field goal, a long shot by Louis Wilkens. The other 10 points were scored by Louis Norris all on free throws.[20] On Friday evening, December 8, 1922, South Side played its first basketball game in the newly completed gymnasium and defeated Shortridge of Indianapolis by a score of 8-7. Alan Fromuth who scored two field goals in the game scored the first basket by a South Side player in the new gymnasium. Don Parker of South Side scored one field goal and Louis Norris scored two free throws. At half time, Shortridge led 3-2. It has been stated that this was the first high school basketball game played in the State of Indiana with glass backboards.[21] The formal dedication of the South Side High School building took place on Sunday, December 10, 1922. The principal address at the dedication ceremonies was delivered by B.J. Burris, State Superintendent of Schools. Additional speakers were Superintendent of Fort Wayne Schools, Louis C. Ward, and Principal Robert C. Harris. Standing at the entrances during the dedication were people distributing circulars denouncing the new South Side structure as unsafe. They declared that those going into the place were risking their lives. This prompted several investigations by the school board and city council. A controversy swirled for a couple of months about the safety of the new South Side High School, but nothing really came of the uproar.[22]

On January 23, 1923, the first basketball game ever played between South Side and Central took place resulting in a 26-22 South Side victory in double overtime. The South Side girls' team made it a double victory winning the preliminary from Central by a score of 25-7.[23] Later in this first basketball season, Central gained revenge by defeating South Side in another double overtime game marking the second meeting between the two rivals. In the 1923 sectional tournament, also referred to as the district tournament, South Side became the first Fort Wayne school ever to win the sectional defeating Central 17-15. One of South Side's earlier victories in the 1923 sectional was a 58-3 route of Huntertown. South Side led at the end of the first half by a score of 26-0.[24]

After winning the sectional basketball tournament, South Side went on to the regional tournament and defeated Garrett in the first game but lost to Warsaw in the regional final by a score of 19-16. Members of South Side's successful first basketball team were Herbert Mayer, Don Parker, Ray Plasterer, Alan Fromuth, Eugene Englehart, Louis Norris, Louis Wilkens, who was team captain, Park Williams, and George Wyss.[25] South Side's first cheerleaders were Paul Hahn, Mary McCurdy and Robert Hanna.[26] In the early years, South Side's athletic teams were known by many different names. They were called the "Kelly Klads," the "Fighting Green," the "Green Wave," the "Wardmen," and various other nicknames since the name "Archers" would not be chosen for several years.[27]

During the first year, Martin Reiner was elected editor-in-chief of the 1923 *Annual*. When South Side first opened, the yearbook had no name but was referred to as "The Annual."[28] At the end of 1922, a contest was held so that a name could be chosen for "The Annual." All of the suggested names were to be submitted by December 15, 1922, so that at the end of 1922 "The Annual" would have a name.[29] As it turned out, several suggested names were submitted and the committee had quite a struggle in selecting the winner. Finally, late in January of 1923, the name "Totem" was unanimously chosen. This name had been suggested by Miss Milocent Work, a South Side Latin teacher. The suggestion by Miss Work came after the committee was deadlocked over some of the other choices which included, "High Life," "Pot Pourri," "Cenci," and "South Sidean."[30]

Music and dramatics have always played a large part in student life at South Side High School and the first year of the school's existence was no exception. Mr. Rolland Schafer directed the music department at South Side for many years. According to the 1923 *Totem*, he had a beautiful tenor voice and an unbounded enthusiasm for his art.[31] The first South Side High School band consisted of eleven musicians, all boys, and was directed by Mr. Schafer. The South Side High School band made its first appearance at the South Side-New Haven baseball game played in the brand-new South Side stadium in the spring of 1923. This first band had no uniforms but plans were already underway for the musicians to perform at football and basketball games the following year and to be decked out in green and white uniforms.[32] The first

SOUTH SIDE'S FIRST CHEERLEADERS

"Chic" Hahn   Mary McCurdy   "Tub" Hanna

clubs organized at South Side High School in the 1922-23 school year were Hi-Y, So-Si-Y, Junior Hi-Y, Math and Science Club, USA Debating Club, Art Club, Varsity Club (later the Lettermen's Club) and South Side's oldest continuous club, Philalethians (later known as Philo). This club, a literary society for second semester sophomore, junior and senior girls, was organized by Miss Elizabeth Demaree in the fall of 1922.[33]

In the spring of 1923, South Side High School was completing its first year and there were the usual end-of-the-year activities. The first senior play entitled, "Clarence," was presented at the Majestic Theater on Friday, April 13, 1923. Leading roles in this play were taken by Evelyn Lewis, Paul Rothert, Ruth Wagner, Paul Hahn, Edna Henderson, Helene Hoffman, Floyd Bergel, Margaret Iler, Harold Sells and Paul Oliver. The play was directed by Vern C. Sheldon of the Sheldon School of Speech and Dramatic Arts. Mr. Sheldon was assisted by Miss Martha Pittenger and Mr. Benjamin Null, head of the South Side English Department.[34] In April of 1923, "The Bells of Beaujolais" was presented at the Central High School auditorium. Dorothy Bolt played the principal role as the countess.[35]

In the spring of 1923, the new South Side stadium was not completed but it was finally leveled and rolled, and the South Side High School-Huntington baseball game was the first athletic contest actually played in the stadium.[36] South Side's first year was complete with such events as the junior prom, senior dance, and graduation. The first junior prom or as it was called "Junior Promenade" was held in the gymnasium on the evening of May 19, 1923. The class colors of purple and white made the gymnasium quite attractive. Paul Hahn's orchestra, the "Terpsichorean Teasers" provided the music.[37] On the afternoon of Tuesday, June 12, 1923, South Side's first commencement was held in which 80 seniors were graduated. The officers of South Side's first graduating class were John Koepf, president; Paul Hahn, vice president; Mary Forker, secretary; and Dorrit Astrom, Paul Rothert and Elizabeth Hadley, social council. The valedictorian of South Side's first graduating class was Vivian Powell and the salutatorian was Beatrice Roush. Eight other students who were selected as "honor students" were Dorrit Astrom, Deane McAfee, Bertha Bandtel, Walter Enz, Ray Krieger, Hilda Schwier, Henry Doenges, and Valette Wellman.[38] When South Side High School celebrated its 25th anniversary in 1947, the *Fort Wayne News Sentinel,* Roto Section, carried a photograph of Vivian Powell, valedictorian of the 1923 class with her daughter Jackie Wilson, who was valedictorian of the 1947 silver anniversary class of South Side.[39]

Between September of 1923 and June of 1926 South Side High School built upon the foundations established during the first year. In the spring of 1923, a young man rode the interurban from Muncie to Fort Wayne getting off at the stop located on Bluffton Road near Broadway. He walked several blocks to the almost-new South Side High School and was quite impressed with what he saw. As he entered the school for his job interview, he was met by the principal, Robert C. Harris, and the superintendent of schools, Louis C. Ward who were ready to embark upon a tour of the building. Invited to join them, the young teacher spent the rest of the afternoon trekking through the school including a rather adventurous trip across the roof. At the end of the afternoon, he was informed that he had been hired. The young man was Ora Davis who joined the South Side faculty beginning in September of 1923 and was to remain for a total of forty-one years serving as teacher, athletic director, and guidance counselor.[40]

Other notable additions to the South Side faculty in September of 1923 were Herman Makey, Mary McCloskey and Pearl Rehorst, all of whom remained on the South Side faculty for periods in excess of twenty-five years. John Hoffman, a graduate of the class of 1933, remembers the themes returned to students by Herman Makey which contained numerous red marks signifying grammatical errors. The students were to correct each grammatical error with no hints or help from Mr. Makey. If these corrections could not be accomplished during class time, the students reported to Mr. Makey after school and made several visits to his desk until each error was corrected. John Hoffman remembers being tardy at many basketball practices because he was waiting in line in Mr. Makey's room to correct his themes.[41] In 1924, Albert Heiny, Emma Kiefer and Olive Perkins joined the faculty and in 1925, among the long tenured

Top Row
(L to R):
Theil, Brubaker,
Gilbert, Weiner,
Fromuth

Middle Row:
Currie, Norris, Wilkens,
Wyss

Bottom Row:
Willson, Rahe

1923-24 BASKETBALL – SECTIONAL AND REGIONAL CHAMPIONS

Top Row
(L to R):
Monroe, Bade, Berlien,
D. Bales, Hadsell

Middle Row:
Baumgartner, Shively,
Dix, Wager, Tannehill,
Mason

Bottom Row:
Schmieder, E. Bales,
Diggs, Minier

1923-24 GIRLS BASKETBALL TEAM

teachers added were Mary Crowe, Georganna Hodgson and Gertrude Oppelt.[42]

The first football game played in the newly completed South Side stadium took place on Saturday, October 13, 1923, when South Side defeated Kendallville by a score of 45-0. The first touchdown ever scored in the stadium took place in the last part of the first quarter when Don Currie, the South Side fullback, returned a punt forty-five yards for the score.[43] An interesting story is related to the first football game in the stadium. Principal Robert Harris indicated that uniforms would be furnished for the band and wanted the band to make a good showing for this first football game. Mr. Harris is quoted as saying, "We must have a band of 50 members this year. Every member who joins the band does not need to know how to play an instrument for lessons will be given free and instruments furnished. We do not know how many of the fifty members in the band actually knew how to play their instruments on the day of that first football game in the stadium.[44] The 1923 football team, the second and last to be coached by Ward Gilbert, did not duplicate the feat of the 1922 team by going undefeated, but did finish with a very respectable six win-two loss record, including a 28-0 victory over Central.[45]

The Central Interscholastic Press Association convened its annual convention on November 30 and December 1, 1923, at the University of Wisconsin in Madison. South Side High School eager to atone for the fiasco which happened the year before when its newspaper was named, "The Best Junior High School Paper in the Nation" sent a delegation to Madison consisting of Rowena Harvey, faculty advisor, Ehrman Kickley, editor-in-chief, Hubert Beck, managing editor, and Zoe Marahrens, city editor. A huge front-page head-line in the *Times*, told the story when it proclaimed, "SS Times Wins Title." In competition with 238 papers representing the best journalistic efforts of high schools in 35 states, the *South Side Times* was named, "The Best High School Paper in the United States.[46] Vivian Crates Logan, a former general manager of the *South Side Times* reminisced about the gigantic victory at Madison in the ten year anniversary issue of the *South Side Times*. She recalled that Miss Harvey sent a telegram to principal Robert C. Harris saying, "We are bringing home the bacon." When Miss Harvey and the staff arrived in town, Mr. Harris was there with the school band, and while the band played, Miss Harvey presented the principal with a slab of bacon.[47]

Sara Davis, wife of long-time faculty member George Robert Davis, recalls that a group of faculty wives and associate members organized the Hesperian Study Club early in 1924. The club was a literary society with an emphasis on book reviews and other literary pursuits. The club was founded by Christeena Thomas, Allison M. Murphy, Ethel R. Langston and Esther Logue. The club survived into the 1990's and celebrated its 70th anniversary in 1994.[48]

The 1923-24 South Side High School basketball team was one of the greatest in school history. This team defeated Central three times and won the sectional tournament for the second year in a row. South Side then defeated Angola and Huntington to become the first Fort Wayne team ever to win the regional, and to take part in the state finals at Indianapolis. In those days, the 16 regional winners all advanced to the state finals as there was no semi-state or super regional level. Unfortunately, South Side lost to Richmond in their first game at the state finals. This great South Side basketball team was made up of Louis Wilkens, who was captain, Louis Norris, Alan Fromuth, Charlie Brubaker, George Wyss, Don Currie, James Willson, William Thiele, Chris Branning, Richard Wiener, and Edward Rahe. Fromuth, Norris and Brubaker received All State honors in 1924. The girls varsity basketball team known as the "Mildredites," named after head coach Mildred Hadsell, had a very successful season in 1923-24. The members of the girls varsity basketball team were Dorris Minier, Evelyn Bales, who was captain, Maxine Schmeider, Katherine Diggs, Dorothy Bales, Dorothy Dix, Clara Wager, Pauline Baumgartner, Cornelia Bade, Alice Mason, Mildred Berlien, Holly Shively, Mary Alice Tannehill, and Mary Monroe.

The 1924 *Totem* was dedicated to Herbert S. Voorhees referred to as "the grand old man of South Side High School." Mr. Voorhees was an original faculty member at South Side who taught Chemistry from the time the school opened until his retirement in 1937.[49] At the time of this *Totem* dedication in

1924, Mr. Voorhees had taught in the Fort Wayne Schools longer than any other teacher. He came to Fort Wayne to teach on April 1, 1901. He had been principal at Fort Wayne High School (Central High School) before requesting assignment as a teacher at South Side when the school opened.[50] For many years, there was a room at South Side High School named the "Voorhees Room" which contained, among other things, a large portrait of Herbert S. Voorhees.

In the fall of 1924, Lundy Welborn replaced Ward Gilbert as football coach. In addition, Mr. Welborn coached the baseball team and started South Side's first track team in the spring of 1925. Lundy Welborn had been a star athlete at Butler University. He remained on the faculty at South Side High School for twenty years and spent fourteen seasons as football coach retiring after the 1937 season. During those fourteen seasons, Mr. Welborn's football teams won a total of 76 games while losing 39 and tying nine.[51] Mr. Welborn coached more football victories than any coach in South Side history. The highlight of Mr. Welborn's first season as football coach was South Side's third consecutive victory over Central, a 46-0 game in which Melvin Richendollar, the South Side fullback, scored five touchdowns. A record crowd of 3,513 people attended the 1924 South Side-Central football game.[52]

During South Side's third year, students continued to attain high academic achievement. In the spring of 1925, all five representatives from the Twelfth Congressional District who entered the state finals of the District Latin Contest were from South Side. Those five students were Helen Clapsattle, Pauline Baumgartner, Franklin Smith, Olive Prine and Esther Hanning. In the District Contest, Esther Hanning's grade was 99.88%, just one-eighth of one percent lower than perfect.[53] At the state contest held in Bloomington, Franklin Smith received a gold medal for winning first prize in his division.[54]

In September of 1925 when South Side High School opened for its fourth year, there was a larger student enrollment but also much more room. The South Side Grade School had vacated the building as Harrison Hill opened. The 1925-26 school year would be an eventful one for South Side. Growing pains would continue to be experienced by the new school, and this would be the last year for principal Robert C. Harris. One of the memorable events of this school year was the announcement that famous John Philip Sousa and his band would play at the South Side gym on October 30, 1925.[55] The Sousa concert was a resounding success with more than 2,000 dollars received. South Side's share of the profits was given to the band fund.[56] 1925 was a banner year for South Side publications. The 1925 *Totem* was awarded "The Best in the United States" by two different national organizations. The *South Side Times* in 1925 was again awarded the coveted title of "Best in the United States." Hubert Beck was editor in chief of the 1925 *Totem* and Pauline Baumgartner was general manager of the *South Side Times*.[57]

Lundy Welborn

The 1925 South Side football team known as the "Fightin Green" had an excellent season winning 7 games. The team won the Wabash Valley Conference title but lost the final game of the season to city rival Central by a score of 7-6. This was the first time that Central had defeated South Side in football.[58] This one-point victory by Central was due in large part to the fact that coach Lundy Welborn decided for disciplinary reasons to hold out star fullback Melvin Richendollar who did not play until the second half.[59] This decision resulted in the temporary firing of Coach Welborn by the school board and a strike by South Side High School students. Coach Welborn was later reinstated. Robert "Nobs" Schopf was elected captain for the 1926 football season and was awarded All State honors at tackle for the 1925 season.

In the autumn of 1925 under the leadership of Alice Patterson, the Girls' Athletic Association (GAA) was organized. A Constitution was drawn up and the officers included Elvah Miller, president, Violet Fell, vice president, Gertrude Brower, secretary, Winifred Englehart, manager of sports, Wilma Kronmiller, sophomore representative, Ruth Bennhoff, freshman representative and Ms. Patterson, treasurer. A point system was adopted whereby a girl received points for her activities. The highest award was a varsity "S" given for receiving 1,000 points. The first GAA letter winners were Elvah Miller, Lillian Springer, Violet Fell, Ruth Watkins and Mary Alice Tannehill. The girls varsity basketball team for the 1925-26 season was made up of Doris Bauer who was captain, Gertrude Brouwer, Gladys Guebard, Virginia Bourns, Cleta Hixon, Nellie Merica, Mildred Koster, Velda Nobles, Winifred Englehart, and Elizabeth Augspurger.

In November of 1925, Philip Greeley, a math teacher and athletic manager of South Side High School, died.[60] In February of 1926, under the leadership of the PTA and school officials, it was announced that Room 86 had been set aside and designated as "The Greeley Room." It would be used largely for social purposes and meetings of the school clubs.[61] Room 86 was in the southwest corner of the school and was one of the rooms vacated by the South Side Grade School. It later became the location of the library when the library was moved from the second floor to the first floor, and the Greeley Room moved to the second floor. The Greeley Room has survived in various locations for over seventy years at South Side, including the renovated South Side building where it exists as a brand-new facility.

Early in 1926, South Side High School began to encounter difficulties with the Indiana State Athletic Association, and in particular with permanent secretary Arthur Trester. In February of 1926, South Side was put on probation by the IHSAA Board. The suspension was due to the fact that a South Side athlete, Noble Sprunger, was ruled ineligible by Mr. Trester. Six basketball games in which he played were forfeited. The decision was based upon the fact that Sprunger's name appeared on the Central High School enrollment list in 1921. South Side maintained that Sprunger should not have been placed on the enrollment books. South Side had affidavits to show that he had not entered a single class at Central during the semester beginning in September of 1921. Despite this, the IHSAA Board placed South Side on probation until June 1, 1927.[62] Following this probation, South Side became embroiled in another feud with the IHSAA which started when principal Robert Harris decided to pay certain sectional and regional basketball officials directly instead of sending the money to Indianapolis so that the IHSAA could pay them. As a result, South Side High School was suspended from the IHSAA for a period of one year and could not schedule any games or athletic events with IHSAA members.

B. The Arrival of R. Nelson Snider

Following the suspension of South Side from the Indiana High School Athletic Association, the school board decided to replace Robert C. Harris as principal. Mr. Harris was succeeded by R. Nelson Snider, a twenty-eight year old native of Delaware County, Indiana. Mr. Snider had been serving as principal at James Smart School and he and Robert Harris traded jobs. Mr. Harris remained at James Smart for twenty years until his retirement in 1946, while Mr. Snider remained at South Side High School for the thirty- seven years. During this time, the names of R. Nelson Snider and South Side High School became almost synonymous. R. Nelson Snider was born January 4, 1898, in the village of DeSoto, Indiana. To answer one of the great puzzles that mystified hundreds of South Side students for decades, the "R" in R. Nelson Snider stands for "Roy." As a boy, Mr. Snider was never called Roy but was always called Nelson. In 1914, Mr. Snider graduated from DeSoto High School at the age of 16, being the youngest member of his graduating class. He then entered Indiana Normal School in Muncie (later Ball State University) for the twelve-week course to obtain his teacher's license. He began teaching in a one-room school house in Delaware County in 1915 when he was 17 years of age. His salary was $2.50 per day; in addition he served as janitor. Mr. Snider received his Bachelors Degree in 1922 and was elected president of the junior and senior classes, as well as serving as captain of the Ball State basketball team for three years. He was also a star on the baseball team.[63] R. Nelson Snider's distinguished career in athletics was a well-guarded secret, because one of his credos as a principal was that athletics should assume its proper place as being subservient to academic excellence in a high school. Mr. Snider came to Fort

R. Nelson Snider

Wayne in 1922 as principal of Jefferson School. In 1923, the principal of Smart School was appointed math supervisor for the Fort Wayne City School System, and Mr. Snider was named principal at Smart School. In discussing R. Nelson Snider, Martha Pittenger, longtime dean of girls at South Side, stated, "He was always so resourceful, skillful and quick in thinking. Any time I had a school problem, he always knew the answer. He solved problems quickly and never got off the track."[64]

In his message to the student body published in the South Side Times of September 8, 1926, Mr. Snider said, "Before us lies the possibility for the greatest year that South Side has ever known. Only by untiring labor and sincere devotion to the school can South Side go on to the position of eminence which is its rightful destination."[65] Some of the outstanding changes brought about by R. Nelson Snider during his first year at South Side

High School were introduction of a new method for determining honor roll students, the establishment of a home room system, the organization and activation of the student council, and the organization of the Booster Club which later played an important part in gaining for South Side membership in the National Honor Society.[66] For those who wish to do a more in depth study on the interesting career of R. Nelson Snider, an excellent source is an unprecedented sixty-four page edition of the *South Side Times* dated May 31, 1963. This voluminous edition of the *Times* was published in honor of Mr. Snider's retirement and contains numerous stories and antidotes.

During the 1926-27 school year, the first year in the principalship of R. Nelson Snider, there was great academic progress at South Side, although the shadow of the IHSAA suspension was somewhat of a deterrent to school spirit. As Ora Davis recalls in his memoirs, the suspension came at a most unfortunate time because the 1926 football team was potentially one of the best ever assembled at South Side. Due to the suspension, both the football and basketball teams, were forced to schedule games with colleges and out-of-state high schools who were not members of the IHSAA. Also forbidden was participation by South Side in the 1927 high school basketball tournament.[67]

The 1926 football team was able to schedule five games and was undefeated although there was a memorable 0-0 tie with Moosehart of Illinois who claimed to be national high school champions. Moosehart was a orphanage established by the Moose Lodge and the game with South Side took place on October 30, 1926 which coincided with the State Moose Convention being held in Fort Wayne. A large crowd gathered at South Side stadium to observe a hard-fought battle which ended in a scoreless tie. The game was featured by numerous booming punts by Wilson McCormick of South Side which kept Moosehart from scoring. Only one touchdown was scored against the 1926 football team during the entire season. It was indeed a shame that such outstanding South Side High School football players such as captain Robert "Nobs" Schopf, South Side's All State tackle and Wilson McCormick were deprived of the opportunity to play other high schools during their senior year.[68] Since the basketball team was also unable to schedule other Indiana high schools, as well as being prohibited from playing in the tournament, they were forced to schedule games with college and semi-pro basketball teams. The South Side varsity basketball team won only six games during the 1926-27 season.[69] Track was the first sport that South Side participated in after being readmitted to the IHSAA. The track stars on the 1927 team were Bill Goudy, Dick Bell, Wilson McCormick and LeRoy Shine. Baseball was dropped in the spring of 1927 in order that more attention might be paid to the track team, although baseball was re-instituted as a sport in 1928 and 1929.[70] While South Side was experiencing difficulties on the athletic field, the *South Side Times* and *Totem* continued to bring honors to the school. In the first four years of the existence of South Side High School, its publications won more championships than any other high school in the country. Charles Rise served as editor of the 1927 *Totem*. The photography staff was made up of Sheldon Hine, later to become a very famous photographer, Robert Borkenstein and Roger Ralston. Robert Thompson served as general manager of the South Side Times and Helen Foellinger served as editor. Mary Graham, a future South Side teacher, served as copy editor during the spring of 1927. During the 1926-27 school year, a guide book entitled, *The Green Book* was published with Helene Foellinger serving as editor in chief. Both Helene Foellinger and Robert Thompson went onto achieve journalistic prominence following their graduation from South Side High School. During the fall of 1926, the Meterites Club was organized by Miss Myra Esarey. This club was the "little sister" organization to Philo and membership was open to freshmen and first semester sophomore girls.[71]

Notable additions to the faculty in the fall of 1926 were Emma Shoup, long-time librarian, and Wilburn Wilson, who would become head of the Social Studies Department. As the decade of the 1920's came to a close, other faculty members arriving at South Side were Susen Peck (1927), Rose Mary DeLancey, Russell Furst, Jake McClure, Lucy Mellen, Paul Sidell, and Grace Welty, all of whom arrived in 1928, and Nell Covalt, Earl Sterner and Pauline VanGorder, who arrived in 1929.[72] Also joining the faculty in 1929 was Louis Briner who was a physical education teacher and director of intramurals. He set up an intramural program which was one of the finest in the nation, and he would continue on the South Side faculty for another twenty-three years until his death during the summer of 1952. Another significant addition to the faculty in 1929 was Dorothy Benner (later Dorothy Benner Rieke) who took over the reigns of the Wrangler's Club and produced many fine public speakers at South Side in the 1930's and 1940's.

During the late 1920's, South Side High School continued to field strong athletic teams. At the 1928 state track meet, Dick Bell became the first South Sider ever to win an individual track title when he finished first in the half-mile run. The 1927 football team won the first title of the new organization known as the Northeast Indiana Conference. Also, South Side produced many football stars, including Bernard Dickey, Norman "Tut" Miner and Martin Ellenwood. The 1928-29 basketball team, the first to be known as the "Green Archers" won the sectionals, regionals, and in 1929, South Side made its second trip to the sixteen team state finals. In the first game of the state finals, South Side defeated Attica but then lost to Indianapolis Tech in the second game. The 1928-29 basketball team was guided by a new coach, Jake McClure, and won twenty-two games. At that time, that was the most games ever won in one season by a South Side basketball team. Among the standout players on the 1928-29 basketball team were Martin Ellenwood, Norman Miner, Bob Mooney, Bernard Dickey, Frank "Yank" Wilson, Sam Fleming, Hub Ralston, Max Baxter, Mark Talmadge and Billy Stults.

On the baseball diamond, South Side continued to field excellent baseball teams which featured Earl Bolyard, who later played for the New York Yankees.[73]   South Side students continued to win academic honors when Helen Dills won first place in the state shorthand contest in 1928.[74]

C. We Become "The Archers"

The two outstanding events of the late 1920's were the establishment of a chapter of the National Honor Society at South Side High School and the selection of the name "Green Archers" as the official school nickname. In late 1928, R. Nelson Snider appointed a faculty committee composed of Herman Makey, chairman, Milocent Work, Herbert S. Voorhees, Earl Murch, and Mrs. Mabel Thorne to select the first students for membership to the National Honor Society. On December 17, 1928, ten graduates of the January class of 1929 became charter members of the Promethean chapter of the National Honor Society. A student assembly was held in the gymnasium for the purpose of presenting the memberships. The first ten students to become members of the National Honor Society at South Side High School were Robert Hickey, Dorothy Rinehart, Grace Coudret, May Jane Newby, Howard Craig, Gertrude Fawley, Lucille Lindeman, Sam Fleming, Rosanna Haven and Dalma Anderson. On May 17, 1929, 13 members of the June graduating class were added. Those students were Edward Grote, Pauline Thompson, Charles Gruenert, Marjorie Wolver, Betty Ward, Thelma Lare, Katherine Pepper, Clarence Bosselman, Wilma Swindler, Mary Graham, Doris Davenport, Ruth Buist and Eleanore Rupnow.[75]

By late 1928, there was growing dissatisfaction among the students and faculty of South Side High School that the school had no official nickname. This was no doubt prompted by the fact that a new high school, namely North Side, had opened in the fall of 1927, and had a nickname, the "Redskins," while Central High School had adopted the nickname of the "Tigers." The South Side Teams were still referred to as the "Fighting Green," "The Kellies," and "Kelly Klads." On November 22, 1928, the South Side Times announced that there was going to be a school wide vote to determine the new nickname.[76] On December 7, 1928, the top three selections were announced. Those selections were Eagles, Green Archers and no new name wanted.[77] On Friday, December 7, 1928, the vote was taken and the results of the final ballot were Green Archers 517 votes, Eagles 200 votes and no new name 152 votes. Consequently, on December 7, 1928, South Side High School officially became the "Green Archers."[78] The first sports stories designating the South Side basketball team as the "Archers" appear in the December 13, 1928, issue of the *South Side Times*. On March 21, 1929, the official trademark of the South Side Archer went on sale for a price of ten cents. The transfer suitable for placement on the windshields of automobiles was circular in shape and about three inches in diameter. On a white background, a kneeling Archer dressed in green is depicted shooting an arrow, and around the edge the words, "South Side Archers" are printed.[79]

1929 Totem

In June of 1929, South Side graduated two hundred twenty-five seniors, which was the largest graduating class up to that time in South Side history.[80] As the 1920's ended, the stock market crashed and what was to be called the "Great Depression" was beginning. Scant attention was paid to this at South Side High School as the events of another school year took precedent. In September of 1929, the *South Side Times* headline proclaimed South Side to be the largest school in the city with an enrollment of 1,500 students.[81] In the autumn of 1929, it was announced that the South Side High School baseball team had been awarded an Northeast Indiana Conference baseball title for the 1929 baseball season.[82] In the South Side Times for the first time on November 21, 1929, appeared the column entitled, "Up and Down Our Inclines" which ran for several decades.[83] As the decade of the 1920's ended, it was announced that Archer football players George Hood and Earl Bolyard had received mention on the All State football team chosen by the United Press.[84]

CHAPTER TWO
1930 - 1939

A. The Depression

As the decade of the 1930's opened, economic conditions and fighting the depression were the top national issues. Later in the decade, attention was devoted to the rise of the Nazi's and Adolf Hitler. At South Side High School, all was serene. The attention of students was focused on the Wrangler's dance to be held after the North Side-South Side basketball game in February of 1930.[1] South Side was the largest high school in town with a total enrollment of 1,564 students .[2] There was great excitement at South Side because eighteen lucky students received free rides in the *News Sentinel's* new airplane named, "The Yankee Clipper."[3] South Side students in 1930 were interested in eating lunch at "Nick's Greasy Spoon" located across the street from the school; they also attended the afternoon tea dances which were organized and hosted by Miss Gertrude Oppelt.

In the autumn of 1930, the Archers' cross-town rival, North Side High School, introduced the era of Friday night football to Fort Wayne when they installed forty powerful flood lights on their football field.[4] South Side was to play its home games on Saturday afternoons for many years to come. Bob Parker, a 1933 South Side graduate, later to become famous as a baseball historian and cartoonist, remembers attending the Saturday afternoon football games and then racing home after the game to catch the final innings of the World Series between the Cardinals and Philadelphia Athletics on the new-fangled device known as the radio.[5] Don Powell, one of the great football players in South Side history, made the 1930 football team as a freshman.[6]

In the fall of 1930, Louis C. Ward, then superintendent of schools, announced a 500,000 dollar building project at South Side High School. If all had gone according to plan, a new addition to the school would have been built on the south side of Gumpper Avenue (now Oakdale) on a piece of land that was bought by the school corporation in the 1920is. The new addition would contain a girl's gym, an auditorium and a swimming pool.[7] This plan did not materialize because of the depression. South Side did eventually get a girl's gymnasium but the proposal in 1930 for a swimming pool was the closest South Side ever came to having that luxury until the construction of the new campus in the 1990's. This land to the south of the school, later the site of an Azar's Drive-In, was traded in 1955 for the land immediately to the east of the school where the addition was built in the late 1950's.

In May of 1931, the "Green Book" was once again revised under the editorial leadership of Elizabeth Yaple.[8] Helene Foellinger had edited the 1927 version of the "Green Book" while David Parrish was the editor in 1929. In March of 1931, a South Side High School freshman, Dan Zehr set a new international record in the one hundred yard backstroke.[9] Zehr later swam in the 1932 Olympics representing the United States and finished in fourth place. Also in 1931, the Greeley Room was moved upstairs along the Calhoun Street corridor, and the library was moved downstairs into the former location of the Greeley Room in the southwest corner of the first floor where it was to remain for several decades. On Friday night, October 30, 1931, South Side played North Side in the first night game ever played by a South Side football team. The game was won by South Side by a score of 20-6. A few weeks previously on October 3, 1931, the South Side football team defeated Bluffton 56-0 at South Side stadium, and for the first time in South Side history, popcorn was sold at the game.[10]

During the 1931-32 school year, an entirely new public speaking program was introduced by Dorothy Benner. The plan provided for interclass debates and extemporaneous speaking contests. The

1932 Commencement

winner of the first extemporaneous speaking contest was Eugene Grant.[11] The depression really caught up with South Side High School in 1932. The school corporation ran out of money to pay teachers and graduation day in 1932 was May 18, rather than the traditional June date. At that time, South Side graduated a class of 316 students, making it the first time in school history that a graduation class contained more than 300 students. In 1932 and 1933, South Side's football teams won a total of 16 of 21 scheduled games, losing only four and tying one. Don Powell and Chet Ensley were placed on the 1933 All State team. The early 1930's also saw great South Side High School track teams under the coaching of Lundy Welborn. In 1932, South Side finished fourth at the state track and field meet. The stars of this team were Jack Fleming, Bob Clymer, and Chet Ensley.[12] In 1933, the Archer track team finished third at the state meet. South Side's half-mile relay team composed of Bob Berry, Roger Pierson, Bill Gyer and Chet Ensley won first place. In addition, Chet Ensley finished second in the 100-yard dash and second in the 220.[13] Herbert Banet, a star in both football and basketball, was the 1933 winner of the King Trophy. Banet later became head basketball coach at Central High School.

In 1933, Melvin Eggers and Jane Beasey played the leads in the senior class play entitled, "The Guest of Honor," while Winfield Moses and Betty Peters won honors in public speaking. Louis Bonsib, a freshman, won an advertising award from "Quill and Scroll."[14] Further academic honors came to South Side on April 21, 1933, at the State Latin Contest held at Indiana University in Bloomington. A gold medal for first place was awarded to Roberta Garton, a junior. Bob Harruff, a freshman, won second place. Third place was presented to Dorothy Fathauer, a sophomore, and Ruth Rohrbaugh received third place in the senior division. Dean S.E. Stout, head of the Latin Department at Indiana University, remarked after the awards had been made, "This is certainly a most unusual occurrence to have one school send down four winners and to have each one receive a medal. It is both a great distinction and honor for South Side High School."[15] At South Side's first Recognition Day on June 9, 1933, a silver cup was given to Sam Rea for writing the best theme in English 6. By the end of the 1932-33 school year, there were 1,848 students in South Side, and conditions were becoming very crowded at the world's largest one story high school.

In September of 1933, Room 65, a former art room, was converted into the Voorhees Room. This room was named after chemistry teacher, Herbert Voorhees, "the grand old man of South Side." In this room hung a large portrait of Mr. Voorhees. The room was to be used, in addition to the Greeley Room, for club meetings.[16] In the fall of 1933, Jack Wainwright arrived as the new music director taking over both the band and the orchestra. Mr. Wainwright was to be a distinguished member of the South Side faculty for a period of ten years and wrote many original compositions, including the South Side Alma Mater. Shortly after Mr. Wainwright's arrival, the membership of the band increased from 50 to 120 members, and the orchestra leaped from 35 members to 60 members.[17] During the 1933-34 school year, South Side continued to excel in journalistic endeavors. Mark Gross wrote an article for the *School Press Review*, and won first place in the east central states in sports writing, first in Indiana in news story and second in the east central United States in editorial. Louis Bonsib won first prize in the United States in an advertising contest. Paul Deal wrote an article which appeared in the national magazine of "Quill and Scroll."[18] As the 1934-35 school year opened, South Side joined other schools in celebrating the Tercentenary which marked the 300th anniversary of the American Public School System which had originated with the founding of the Boston Latin School in 1635. In the public speaking area, Manual Rothberg and Robert Klopfenstein won state titles. The general managers of the *Times* were Wayne Bender, John Bremmer and Louis Bonsib.

In 1935, Mr. Earl Murch, head of the Business Department, entered his advanced students in the Indiana State Commercial Contest. South Side had not entered the contest for almost ten years, and this year it was done solely for the sake of finding out how South Side students ranked with other commercial departments. South Side won the initial or mass contest which was taken by the entire shorthand classes of all schools entered. South Side was then qualified to enter the final stage of the contest, and three members of the class, Anna Brumbaugh, Alma Nitsche and Dorothy Fathauer were chosen to represent the school in the state meet at Ball State Teacher's College in Muncie. Dorothy Fathauer won the first place individual award. The South Side team won first place in the State Shorthand Contest.[19]

On the basketball court, the 1934-35 basketball team, the last to be coached by Jake McClure, had a very successful season winning 16 and losing four. The Archers repeated as sectional champions and went to the finals of the regional before losing to Berne. The members of this 1934-35 varsity basketball team were Bob Nelson, Brower George, Gene Jackson, Bob Symonds, Jim Hilgemann, Joe Close, Hooty Hall, Jim Ellenwood, Ed Ginn and Paul Lohse. The reserve basketball team under the tutelage of assistant coach Bill Geyer (still a student and later to be a teacher and coach at South Side), enjoyed a very successful season winning fourteen and losing only four. Among the members of the reserve team were Don Reichert, Carl Hall and John Hines, all were to become future South Side basketball stars.[20] The winners in the freshman-sophomore speech contest in 1934-35 were from the freshman class. They were Kathleen Whitmer, Janet Hartman, Joan Bonsib and Dalton McAlister destined to become one of the great speakers and orators in South Side High School history.[21] In 1935, two South Side girls, Ruth Bormuth and Dorothy Turflinger, compiled a brief history of the school, and they noted that there were 1,914 students enrolled at South Side and 20 of the original faculty members were still teaching at the school.[22]

In September of 1935, Mary Pocock became the first South Side graduate to return as a faculty member. She had graduated from South Side in 1926. Upon her arrival as a teacher, Miss Pocock stated that she had noticed many changes at South Side. She indicated that when she was a student, the library was upstairs where the Greeley Room "is now," and the Greeley Room was downstairs occupying the same location that the library "now uses."[23] Another new faculty member arriving at South Side in the autumn of 1935 was Burl Friddle who became the varsity basketball coach succeeding Jake McClure. Mr. Friddle who was to remain at South Side for seven years became famous as the first coach to lead South Side to a state basketball championship. He had been a member of the "Franklin Wonder Five" which had won three state championships in the early 1920's. He had also coached Washington High School to the state championship in 1930. In January of 1936, Stuart Monroe, a graduate of the

Bob Parrish   Paul Deal   Mark Gross

"We're on Our Way"

—*Franklin D. Roosevelt*

class of 1925, was hired as a manual arts teacher, thus becoming the second South Side graduate to return as a faculty member.[24] George Robert Davis, a graduate of the class of 1952 and long-time faculty member, compiled a list of all of the South Side students who later returned as faculty members. This list includes more than forty individuals. In February of 1936, the first in a series of high school variety radio programs was presented by South Side on Station WOWO. The program opened with the South Side Chorus singing, "Cheerio" the school pep song which was written by Jack Wainwright.[25]

On May 13, 1936, Dalton McAlister won first place in the state Rotary speech contest held at Lafayette, Indiana. On the same day, one of the richest traditions in South Side history had its beginning. On May 13, 1936, South Side High School held its first Ivy Day.[26] Ivy Day is a South Side tradition that has continued unbroken for more than sixty years. The first Ivy Day was somewhat different than its successors because it was a joint project of the junior-senior class, and the junior class elected the Ivy Queen.[27] The senior committee members were Ruth Rose, Richard Strasser, Jim Sweet, Anna Bremer and Myron Jones. Junior committee members were Bob Storm, Jim Dern, Bud Theye, Richard Rastetter and Ruth Garrison. The ivy was presented by Manual Rothberg, and the ivy was accepted for the school by principal R. Nelson Snider. The first Ivy Day Queen was Ruth Garrison, a junior, who was elected by members of her class.[28] In all Ivy Days starting with 1937, the queen has been a member of the senior class.

The editor of the 1936 *Totem* was Louis Bonsib. In this *Totem*, we see a photograph of a young freshman boy by the name of Bill Blass lying on the grass in front of the school. As we know, this is the famous Bill Blass who went on to become a world renown clothing designer. Among the yell leaders during the 1935-36 school year was Walker "Bud" Mahurin who became an air ace during World War II shooting down numerous German and Japanese planes.[29] One of the new clubs organized during the 1935-36 school year was the Safety Council. On November 13, 1935, a large safety assembly was held at South Side, and Sergeant Custer Dunifon of the police department spoke on the importance of safety.[30] Sergeant Dunifon, of course, later became the famous Captain Dunifon who worked with dogs and gave safety talks in the schools during the 1940's.

On the gridiron, South Side continued to field excellent football teams. Jim Ellenwood and Fred Ostermeyer were placed on the All City team for 1935 and team captain Fred Nye was chosen as a member of the Second All City team. The 1936 football team started with a ten-day training session at Camp

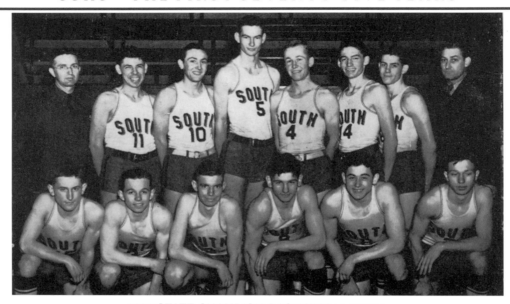

1938 STATE CHAMPION BASKETBALL TEAM
Reading from left to right - Front Row: LeRoy Cook, John chedester, Dale Hamilton, Bob Bolyard, Dick Frazell, Harold Kitzmiller.
Top Row: Ora Davis, Don Hire, Don Beery, Jim Glass, Johnny Hines, Frank Belot, Jim Roth, Coach Burl Friddle.

Crosley. This team won the city championship for the fourth time in five years. They also won the Northeast Indiana Conference title. In addition, they accomplished what no other South Side team had ever done (or has since done) by defeating a strong Mishawaka team 9-7 as a 27-yard field goal by Kenny Miller proved to be the margin of victory. Five members of this team, namely Don Faux, Harold Benz, Bud Feichter, Nelson Miller and James Dern were named to the All City team. Dern was named All City captain and also was placed on the All State team. Bud Feichter led this team in scoring with 42 points. [31] Burl Friddle's first two South Side High School basketball teams lost in the sectionals to Central in both 1936 and 1937. Central went to the state finals in both of these years. Coach Friddle's 1936-37 basketball team had an excellent year, losing only three games. At one point, they won nine in a row. The leading scorers were John Hines, Carl Hall and Don Reichert. During this period, Louis Briner continued his strong intramural program. Some of the sports included in intramurals were bowling, tumbling, basketball, tag football, volleyball, cross country, horse shoes and softball.

When the 1936-37 school year opened, there were still 20 teachers who had been members of the faculty when South Side first opened its doors in 1922. At the conclusion of this school year, two of those original faculty members, namely Martin Rothert, head of the Foreign Language Department, and Herbert Voorhees, the "grand old man of South Side" would retire. By 1937, the South Side High School library boasted a circulation of 6,247 books and 1,880 pamphlets and a yearly circulation of 31,715 documents. [32]

On April 10, 1937, South Side High School had control of Westinghouse Radio Station WGL. This was the so-called "South Side Day on the radio." Those who announced on South Side's Day on the air were John DeYoung (later to become an announcer for Station WGL), Joe Bex, Dalton McAlister, John Jackson, John Edwards, Bob Storm, Herman Rutkowski and Richard Rastetter. Later that month, Dalton McAlister won the state declamation contest held at Franklin College. [33] In commenting on the prospects for the 1937-38 basketball season, the *Totem* stated that Coach Friddle would not have to worry about the lack of experienced players. The *Totem* uttered these words, "Starting practices early before the beginning of the 1937-38 season, Coach Friddle will start the development of the squad which all of South Side hopes will follow the trail of the old cry, 'on to state.' How prophetic were these comments from the 1937 *Totem*.

All eyes on Wonder-boy Glass   Cowboy Friddle and R. Nelson proudly display the trophy   Bobby Bolyard shoots for the basket   Hamilton scores again   tip-off in the final game   another snap of that decisive battle   heads up   the coach gives his final advice   our enthusiastic Archers in the Butler Field House   more boosters   after the final gun was sounded in the Muncie game.

THE WINNAHS!

B. State Champs

In the late 1930's, war clouds were gathering in Europe and the Orient. South Side High School was poised to enter one of its golden ages in academic and athletic achievement. Among the teachers added to the South Side faculty in the autumn of 1937 were Alice Keegan, Lucy Osborne, Stanley Post, Ernest Walker and Dorsa Yoder. Mabel Fortney joined the faculty in 1936. All of these teachers remained at South Side for at least twenty-five years. In 1936, the Indiana High School Athletic Association created a new level in the state basketball tournament, then known as the super regional, now known as the semi-state. Before 1936, all sixteen regional winners had gone to the state finals in Indianapolis. The Fort Wayne regional winner was routed through the Muncie super regional since Muncie had the largest arena in the northeast part of the state seating more than 8,000 people. Until 1938, no large Indiana city had ever claimed the state basketball title. The championship had been won by teams from small towns or from mid-size cities such as Muncie and Anderson.

In 1937-38, Burl Friddle assembled his third basketball team at South Side. This team lost only three games and won its first sectional title since 1935 by defeating arch rival Central.[34] Following the Archer's victory in the regionals, their first at that level since 1929, they headed to the Muncie Super Regional as one of the final 16 teams. In the afternoon games of the 1938 Muncie Super Regional, South Side defeated Sheridan while Muncie Central defeated Kendallville. This set the stage for a showdown

between the Muncie Central Bearcats, odds on favorites to win the 1938 state high school basketball championship, and the South Side Archers. By 1938, the state high school basketball tournament was routinely broadcast on radio. Handling the play- by-play duties were John Hackett (predecessor of Hilliard Gates) and Gunnar Elliot who broadcast the game back to Fort Wayne through the facilities of the local Westinghouse station WGL. For those devotees of Archer athletic history who desire a thrilling experience, tape recordings of the 1938 Super Regional final against Muncie are available. This writer wishes to thank George Robert Davis for making available his tapes of the 1938 Muncie Super Regional, as well as the 1938 state championship game.

In the Muncie game, the South Side starting line-up was Bob Bolyard and Dale Hamilton at forwards, six foot, ten inch Jim Glass (a giant in those days) at center and guards Jim Roth and John Hines. The first period ended with the score South Side 11, Muncie Central 4. In the second quarter when a time out was called by Muncie with the score South Side 15, Muncie 7, the announcer said, "You folks who missed this one should be here. This is a wild house." The Muncie field house was filled to its capacity of 8,500 people. Included in this number were 1,900 people from Fort Wayne cheering on the Archers. The first half of the game ended with the surprising result that South Side was leading Muncie by a score of 18-14. At one point in the third quarter, South Side stretched its lead to nine points but Muncie then made a comeback. As the gun sounded to end the third quarter, South Side led Muncie 29-24. With four minutes to go in the final quarter, things looked bad for the Archers. Hines had already fouled out of the game and three South Side starters, Hamilton, Bolyard and Glass each had three fouls (in those days you were only allowed four fouls.) With less than four minutes to go in the final quarter, Muncie had crept within one point of the Archers. Muncie finally tied the game at 33-33 with somewhere between one and two minutes to play. The announcers in 1938 had to talk in terms of "somewhere between one and two minutes" because the clocks of that era did not tell precisely how much time was left. They were structured only in terms of minutes and did not include seconds. The crowd went wild when Muncie tied the game, but a basket by Harold Kitzmiller gave South Side a 35-33 lead with a minute or less to be played. A field goal by Jim Roth then made the score South Side 37, Muncie 33 with less than a minute to play. As the gun went off, the excited announcer yelled, "South Side goes to state!"[35]

For the first time in school history, South Side advanced to the final four of the high school basketball tournament. Previous Archer teams in 1924 and 1929 had advanced to the 16-team state finals. The teams who comprised the final four in addition to South Side were Columbus, Bedford (who had beaten South Side during the regular season), and Hammond. In the first afternoon game, South Side defeated Columbus while Bedford lost to Hammond. In the championship game, Hammond jumped out to a 7-0 led over South Side. At the end of the first quarter, Hammond led 9-4. By the end of the first half, South Side held a two-point lead at 17-15. In the third period, Hammond took a four- point lead but a basket by John Hines tied the game at 24-24. In the third quarter, South Side overtook Hammond and early in the fourth quarter was enjoying a 32-28 lead. With a little less than two minutes to go, the South Side margin had been cut to 32-30. Jim Roth then scored making it South Side 34, Hammond 30. Hammond immediately scored cutting the margin to two points with less than two minutes to go. South Side was able to stall out the last several seconds of the game and as the gun went off, announcer Gunnar Elliott said, "Fort Wayne is the state champion and nothing else." Burl Friddle, South Side's coach, interviewed after the game said, "We're sure happy to bring a championship to Fort Wayne. The people can be proud of the boys that played for South Side High School tonight."[36]

The South Side victory in the high school championship game prompted a celebration which up to that time had never been equalled in the city of Fort Wayne. On the Saturday night after the victory, bon fires were built and crowds gathered in the streets as the city went wild. At South Side, a huge bonfire was built to celebrate the victory. The crowd ebbed downtown in a snake dance and there was also a bon fire on the courthouse square.[37] The members of the 1938 state championship basketball team were Bob Bolyard, Dale Hamilton, Jim Glass, Jim Roth, John Hines, Dick Frazell, Harold Kitzmiller, Frank Belot, Don Berry, John Chedester, LeRoy Cook, and Don Hire. Bolyard, Hamilton and Glass were selected to the All State team.

Could South Side repeat as state basketball champions in 1939? If regular season play was any indication, the Archers had to be the odds on favorites to capture the 1939 state title. The 1938-39 South Side basketball team posted the only undefeated regular season in school history. The team did, however, lose two games in a holiday tournament at Hammond. The 1938-39 basketball team opened defense of their state title with a sectional win over Central, defeated Leo and Decatur and finally North Side to win the sectional championship. In the first game of the regional at Huntington, they defeated Redkey. In the regional final, they were the victims of one of the most stunning upsets in Indiana basketball history losing to the Ossian Bears 42-28.[38] The members of the highly successful 1938-39 basketball team were Bob Bolyard, Don Berry, Jim Glass, Don Hire, Carl Hall, Ralph Hamilton, Bob Hines, John Chedester, LeRoy Cook and Carl "Blackie" Braden. Bob Bolyard was selected for the All State team.

Even the so-called minor sports received their share of glory during this golden age of South Side athletics in the late 1930's. The golf team won the Northeast Indiana Conference championship in 1937, 1938 and 1939. In 1937, Bud Theye set a school record of 73 at the Foster Park golf course. The South Side tennis team, coached by Stanley Post, had a three-year record in 1938, 1939 and 1940 of twenty-three wins and no losses. They were led by Dick Doermer and Paul Dammeyer.[39] South Side's football teams of the late 1930's did not share in the victories experienced by the other athletic teams. Lundy Welborn's final team, the 1937 squad, won only one game. At the end of that season, Mr. Welborn retired as coach after 14 seasons during which his teams won more games than those coached by any other Archer football mentor. The coaching reigns for the 1938 football season were assumed by Bill Moss whose first Archer team lost all of its ten scheduled games, the first time in school history that this had taken place. Coach Moss's second team in 1939 did achieve a respectable five win, two loss, one tie record. Even though the Archer football teams of the late 1930's experienced few victories, there were some outstanding individual players, including Jim Phelps and Kenny Moeller who achieved All City honors in 1937. Other outstanding South Side gridders of this period were LeRoy Cook, David Roth, Byron McCammon and Tom Moorhead, who later played on some of the great Bo McMillin teams at Indiana University and set an NCAA record for blocked punts which still stands. Girls' athletics continued to flourish at South Side in the late 1930's. Irene Neimeyer, a member of the class of 1938, accumulated more than 1,500 points in GAA activities and earned her varsity letter.[40]

Athletic achievement was not the only showcase for South Side students in the late 1930's. The editor of the 1938 *Totem* was Joan Bonsib who was the second link in an unprecedented family chain of *Totem* editors. Louis Bonsib was editor of the 1936 *Totem* , his brother, John Bonsib, was editor of the 1941 *Totem* and younger brother, Richard Bonsib, was editor of the 1949 *Totem*. Dalton McAlister, referred to as the "ace of aces" of Archer speakers won numerous local, state and national public speaking contests in the late 1930's.

Rosemary Lehman won the state Latin contest at Indiana University in 1937.[41] In 1938, victory was repeated for South Side in the state Latin contest as June Flaig, a freshman, and Betty Garton, a senior, both captured state championships.[42] South Side achieved a three-peat in the state Latin contst when Violet Steinbauer, a sophomore, won at the state level at Indiana University in 1939.[43] South Side's success continued in the public speaking arena as the school swept major honors in all divisions at the state declamation contest held at Franklin College in 1939. Winners at this state contest were Bob Safer, Bill Newhard, Jeanette Warren, and Helen Wiehe. All of these students, along with Tom Gallmeyer, who had won numerous state and national speaking titles in 1938 and 1939, competed in the national contest held in the summer of 1939 in Beverly Hills, California.[44]

C. Growing Pains – We Add A Second Floor

In the late 1930's, South Side High School was experiencing growing pains. The school population for several years had been approximately 2,000 students who were attempting to navigate in a building that was built for 1,500. By 1937, the study hall was overflowing and the Greeley Room had been turned into a secondary study hall.[45] At the same time, stories began appearing to the effect that South Side would add a second floor and would build the long-sought auditorium.[46] When South Side students arrived for the opening of school in September of 1938, they were greeted with improvements which included a radio public address system and an almost-completed second story with new classrooms There had also been renovation on the first floor. The students also greeted new faculty members including track coach, George Collyer and social studies teacher Clyde Peirce.

Included in the massive construction project was the building of stairways in the southeast and southwest corners of the building. These were the first stairways built in South Side High School. The building of these stairways eliminated the need for the incline located at the south end of the building by the biology room. Many generations of Archers observed the locked door at the head of this incline which was no longer needed after the 1938 renovation. The Greeley Room which had been moved from the first floor to the second floor in the early 1930's was moved for a third time farther north on the second floor to make way for expanded administrative offices. In the new Greeley Room, a stage was added as well as a kitchenette.[47] Two study halls were constructed on the second floor. Neither of those new study halls would be used extensively in the 1938-39 school year.[48] The reason for the two new study halls was that phase two of the renovation project to be started in 1939 would feature the tearing out of the first floor study hall and replacing it with an auditorium which would seat 4,000 to 5,000 people. In addition, music and art rooms would be built.[49] This was yet another false alarm concerning the construction of the badly needed auditorium which did not take place until the 1970's. Phase two of the South Side renovation project of the late 1930's never took place.

The new public address system was installed in late September of 1938. The first person to speak over this new public address system was principal R. Nelson Snider. He spoke to some of the social studies classes to inform them that Adolf Hitler, dictator of Germany, had summoned the leaders of Italy, France and Great Britain to an important four-power conference at Munich (Germany) to try to settle the Czechoslovakian dispute. The public address system made it possible to broadcast daily bulletins during homeroom period instead of the mimeographed daily bulletins that had been in existence for years.[50] As the 1930's ended, Hitler invaded Poland, and World War II broke out in Europe. There is no mention of these events in the *South Side Times*.

In September of 1939, the big event at South Side High School was installation of lights in the football stadium. These lights were installed by Central High School so that the Tigers could play their home football games on Friday evenings instead of Saturday afternoons.[51] The result of Central's installation of lights at South Side stadium was that for many years, well into the 1950's, South Side played its home football games on Saturday afternoons, and the Archer's first night appearance in its own stadium was as a visiting team. Some items of national news did appear in the *South Side Times*. In October of 1939, there is a story about Sam Rae, a graduate of the class of 1935, and his recent trip abroad. Because of the trouble in Europe, Sam's trip was cut short. The article tells about an encounter that Sam and some of his University of Pennsylvania classmates had with members of Hitler's Gestapo near a German plane factory.[52]

As the 1930's ended, the entire front page of the *Times* was covered with an ad from the South Side Grill celebrating its third anniversary. This grill was owned and operated for many years by Herb Kenworthy. Among the menu items shown in this 1939 full-page ad were T-bone steak for 70 cents, hamburger steak for 35 cents and a baked ham dinner for 40 cents.[53]

SHELDON HINE

Following is quoted in the 1936 Totem: "This South Side alumnus who has done much for this year's Totem. He has made possible some of the beautiful feature photographs in this book. Mr. Hine is a modest person and won't admit of his greatnes. Nevertheless, he has and certainly will continue to bring fame in photographic circles to Fort Wayne."

RIDING ON AIR

AS SHADOWS LENGTHEN

Freedom

CHAPTER THREE
1940-1949

A. Archer Green Goes to War

As the decade of the 1940's began, Adolf Hitler completed his conquest of Poland. World War II had officially started, but the early months of 1940 saw the two opposing armies in Western Europe viewing each other over a series of fortifications such as the Maginot Line and not doing much real fighting. These early months of 1940 were known as the "phony war." Thoughts of war were far from the minds of the students at South Side High School in the opening weeks of 1940. Jim Murphy, a senior, represented South Side in the state oratorical contest at Wabash College on February 10, 1940.[1] Miss Adelaide Fiedler organized a new club known as the Junior XYZ's.[2] The question foremost in the minds of South Siders in those early weeks of 1940 was not what would Adolf Hitler do, but, "would South Side High School win its second state basketball title in three years?"

Coach Burl Friddle's 1939-40 basketball team won 17 out of 20 games during the regular season. Following this highly successful season, they won their third consecutive sectional tournament, the regional tournament and for the second time in three years went to the Super Regional at the Muncie Field House.[3] South Side won its afternoon game at the Super Regional defeating Garrett and met New Castle in the night game; the winner would go to the final four in Indianapolis. With less than a minute gone in the third quarter and the Archers trailing the New Castle Trojans 25-17, the field house lights mysteriously went out. The game was held up for 34 minutes until electricians repaired the lights. Following resumption of the game, the Archers staged a miraculous rally and defeated New Castle 39-37. Ralph Hamilton, a member of the 1940 All State team, and later an All American at Indiana University scored 22 of South Side's points.[4] For the second time in three years, South Side was going to the final four in Indianapolis! Unfortunately, the Archers were defeated by Mitchell 26-23 in the first afternoon game.[5] The members of this highly successful 1939-40 basketball team were Ralph Hamilton, Don Hire, Bob Hines, Carl "Blackie" Braden, Keith Spiker, Dick Doermer, LeRoy Cook, Ralph Shimer, Gus Feistkorn, and Brice Augsburger.[6] The conclusion of the 1939-40 basketball season completed a miraculous three-year period during which Coach Burl Friddle's Archer basketball teams won three sectional titles, two regional titles, two super regional titles and one state championship. During this period, South Side won 32 consecutive basketball games on its home floor, and won 23 games in the state tournament while losing only two.[7]

South Side's 1940 track team, under Coach George Collyer, had an outstanding season upsetting the favored North Side Redskins to win the sectional. They also won the NEIC title and finished fifth at the state track meet. Outstanding performers on this 1940 track team were LeRoy Cook, Chuck Close, Arden Altman, Rudy Wuttke, Ernie Vogel, David Roth, Bill Miller, Gus Feistkorn, Jim Worman, Arthur Parry, Ralph Shimer, Bob Adams, Paul Fremion and Ronald Duiser.[8] The 1940 tennis team coached by Stanley Post and featuring outstanding individual stars Dick Doermer and Paul Dammeyer finished its fourth consecutive undefeated season and won the NEIC conference title.

By the end of the 1939-40 school year, the war news from Europe was commanding more and more attention. Rev. Charles M. Houser was a guest speaker at the Social Science Club and spoke on "Conditions in Europe."[9] The Travel Club which took "fantasy" trips to various foreign locations decided that "because many of our foreign friends were suffering in the black outs, we would stay at home this year."[10] The senior play of the class of 1940 was entitled, "She Got Away With It." It was a story about two twins, and appropriately starred June McAlister and Joyce McAlister, talented Archer twins in the title roles.[11] The South Side band, directed by Jack Wainwright, took a ten-day concert tour through Ohio and Pennsylvania during the spring of 1940.[12]

In the autumn of 1940, Mr. Lester Hostetler, who was to serve at South Side for many years, joined the faculty as director of vocal music. Prior to the arrival of Mr. Hostetler, Jack Wainwright had directed both instrumental and vocal music.[13] Another new addition to the faculty in 1940 was Wayne Gift who replaced Bill Moss as football coach. Mr. Moss left South Side to take the head coaching job at Shurtleff College in Alton, Illinois.[14] Coach Gift's 1940 football squad enjoyed a successful season winning five and losing two.[15] Bill Siebold, Ralph Shimer and Russell Dickson were named to the All City team.[16] In 1941, for the first time in several years, South Side's basketball team did not win the sectional tournament as they were defeated by Central in the first game of the sectionals. This team did produced some outstanding individual players, including Bob Hines, Gus Feistkorn, Chuck Close, Ralph Shimer and Dallas Zuber. The intramural sports program continued to flourish under the direction of Louis Briner. In 1924, South Side only had seven intramural sports, but by the 1940-41 season, approximately 20 different types of athletic competition were open to boys.[17] In the Girls Athletic Association directed by Mrs. Alice Dean, (later Alice Keegan), the freshman tennis title was captured by Gloria Cadorette, the sophomore tennis title by Marian Faux, the junior title by Betty Hargan and the senior title by Jeanne Smith. In the finals, Marian Faux won the school title.[18]

In 1941, for the first time in Wranglers history, a radio contest was held. The preliminaries were presented over the radio system at South Side while the finals were held at Westinghouse over a station hookup. Those who competed in the finals held at the radio station were Bob Robinson, Bob Young, Bob Safer, Bud Lampton, Fred Collins (later to become a famous radio and television announcer), Byron

Left ro right: Marge Dyer, Social Council; Miss Dorothy Magley, Adviser; Marge Sheldon, Social Council; Mr. Paul Sidell, Adviser; and Dick Theye, Social Council.
Seated in car: June Flaig, Vice-President; Becky Abbett, Secretary; and Jim McClure, President.

R. Nelson Snider and Major Walker M. "Bud" Mahurin.

Teacher Francis Fay in the South Pacific.

Singer and Bill Bone.[19] Jim McClure, president of the senior class, competed in the national oratory contest held at Lexington, Kentucky in 1941 and also placed first in the annual Kiwanis declamation contest held on March 25, 1941.[20] As Archer students returned to South Side in the fall of 1941, they did not know that within 90 days, their lives and the lives of all of their fellow citizens would be changed forever. The 1941 football team, which was the second and last team to be coached by Wayne Gift (he enlisted in the United States Navy), had another successful season winning five games, losing two and tieing one. The outstanding player on the 1941 football team was Ralph Shimer, one of South Side's truly great athletes. In a night game played at the Butler Bowl before more than 6,000 fans, South Side defeated Cathedral of Indianapolis 19-0 as Shimer scored 18 of South Side's 19 points. In the Garrett game won by South Side 66-0, Shimer scored 30 points. The final football game of the 1941 season ended with a nine-six South Side victory over Hammond Tech. Shimer kicked a 35 yard field goal in the first quarter to provide the margin of victory.[21]

On Thursday evening, December 4, 1941, the annual Junior Banquet was held. Among the songs sung were, "Keep the Home Fires Burning," "Til We Meet Again," "Fight On You South Side Archers," and "From Taps Til Reveille." On Friday evening, December 5, 1941, Miss Leona Jolly, a recent arrival from England, spoke to the Social Science Club and told about her experiences during the bombing raids in 1939.[22] On Saturday night, December 6, 1941, Archer couples danced until 11:30 p.m., to the music of Johnny Rathert's Orchestra at "The Christmas Tree Twirl" sponsored by the 1500 Club in Room 170.[23] In the early morning hours of Sunday, December 7, 1941, as many exhausted Archers slept dreaming pleasant memories of "The Christmas Tree Twirl," 300 miles from the island of Oahu, Japanese pilots were twirling the propellers of their planes in preparation for the sneak attack that would "live in infamy." On Sunday, December 7, 1941, the Japanese bombed Pearl Harbor, and the following week the United States entered World War II against Germany and Japan. For the next four years, the war effort was to be the number one priority of all citizens of the United States including the students of South Side High School. Winning the war and the "war effort" became the main objective at South Side and everywhere else in the United States. For a period of four years, World War II completely transformed South Side High School.

South Side's first death in World War II was Captain Howard McCurdy. He was a graduate of the class of 1925 and was killed in action in the Philippines on January 6, 1942.[24] Early in 1942, South Side held its first air raid drill. In the same year, industrial arts students, under the direction of Joe Plasket, prepared model airplanes to help the Navy drive for 500,000 planes a year for airplane identification.[25] Three members of the South Side faculty, Ernest Walker, Wayne Gift and Francis Fay departed for military service.[26] In addition to these three faculty members, 2,070 students or former students, of South Side High

You in the War Effort

The South Side Times

"For Green and White With Main and Might"   All-American--N. S. P. A.; Medalist--C. S. P. A.; International Honor Rating--Quill and Scroll

Vol. XXIII.--No. 12.   South Side High School, Fort Wayne, Indiana, Thursday, December 7, 1944   Price Ten Cents

New Type Reception To Include Parents Planned By Seniors

To Be Held November 29
From 7:30 To 9:30 P. M.
In Room 170

A new type of Senior Reception to include parents has been arranged for Wednesday, November 29, from 7:30 to 9:30 o'clock in Room 170 by officers and advisors. In previous years this reception has been for the seniors alone but this year parents are invited so that they may be now announced earlier in the semester. A program of ....

Meterite Club Names Victors

Pat Seibert and Jackie Wilson were the two winners in the original short story contest held by Meterites in the Greeley Room on October 31. The judges were Mary Belle Hawyer, Sally Hanes, and Anne Waterfield. Other girls who read their stories at the meeting are Rosemary Beck and Mary Warner. Pat Seibert wrote

Makey's Son Gets Medal

Die For Country

Richard Cadorette
Clarence Edward Cremer
Mark Hall
Houston Hicks
John Hogan
George Orr

These names were omitted from the list published last week of ex-South Siders who gave their lives in this war. If any teachers or pupils have any other names, they are asked to please turn them in to the office or the Times room.

$1,000,000 Mark To Be Passed At End Of Bond Rally Today

School Sales Tuesday Reach $189,285.25 With Two Days To Go, An Amount Guaranteeing $1,135,711;
All Names Of War Dead And 1199 Servicemen Drawn

That the Bond Rally will exceed $1,000,000 was assured Tuesday morning when pledges of $189,285.25 doubled the original goal of $85,000 and passed the second goal of $120,000.

With Harry G. Hogan, president of the Dime Bank, doubling the amount, and James H. Haberly, president of the First Federal Loan and Savings Company, matching these two amounts a sum of $1,135,711.50 in

Harry G. Hogan Will Double School Sales At Rally,
James H. Haberly To Match Both; Charles Buesching, Mayor Baals, M. J. Abbett To Speak

Mr. Harry G. Hogan, president of the Dime Bank and the man who will double the Archers' Bond Rally sales, will speak today at the grand finale of the rally to be held in the form of an assembly immediately after the home room period, in the gym. Mr. James H. Haberly, president of the First Federal Loan Company, who will match South Side's purchases and Mr. Hogan's double purchases will also ....

Tribute Is Paid To Twenty-nine Who Gave Lives For Country

All twenty-nine ex-South Siders, who have sacrificed their lives for their country, were signed for by purchases of $1,000 or more in War Bonds by Tuesday ....

School were in military service during World War II. Fifty-four South Siders (one woman and 53 men) were killed during the Second World War.[27] One South Side student, Major Walker "Bud" Mahurin, a graduate of the class of 1937, was shot down over France in 1944 after having completed more than 85 dangerous missions. At one time, Major Mahurin was the leading air ace of the 8th Air Force. On the same day that he was reported missing, he had shot down his 21st German plane.[28] Mahurin was later rescued by the French underground and smuggled back to England. He later transferred to the Pacific theater where he shot down several Japanese planes.

While many Archers wore miliary uniforms and participated in the front-lines of the war effort, the typical South Side student fought the important battle of the home front during World War II. To effectively participate in the war effort, Principal R. Nelson Snider completely reorganized the curriculum of South Side High School. To coincide with pre-induction training required by the armed forces mechanical and electrical courses were covered in the physics department. Specialized instruction and the fundamentals of radio, were also covered. A special physical fitness program was introduced. All junior and senior boys who were physically fit and who were not working at some specific job more than 25 hours per week were required to take a strenuous physical fitness class. Since the needs of the armed forces were for people who were trained in math, a refresher course in math brought all students up to date.

Arrangements were made to give students credit for jobs outside the school in war industry plants. The female population of South Side was not neglected in the war effort and the curriculum revision. The induction of men into the armed forced made the use of girls in industry necessary. Twelve B girls were given an intensive course in shop work, blueprint reading and shop math in order to prepare them for the shop methods and procedure which would be needed in local factories. In home economics classes, emphasis was upon training for home duties and nursing. Edith Crowe taught special courses in first aid. The students were also offered the opportunity to send their old *Times* copies to men in service who had graduated from South Side. All of those whose addresses were known received the *Times*, in addition to an occasional letter. Another sacrifice called for "walking dates" since gas was rationed and dad wouldn't let junior use the car very often. During summer vacations, students participated in their own victory gardens as members of the "Crops Corps."[29]

Rowena Harvery working on the railroad.

Bond Rally raises over $2,000,000

B-25 Purchased by South Siders

To meet manpower shortages caused by the war, Fort Wayne called upon many Archer students and teachers to work after school in its industries. As principal of South Side, R. Nelson Snider served as middle man between the person seeking an employee and the student seeking employment. Students were urged not to work at night since no high school student could hold down two jobs without seriously neglecting one. Usually, students who worked late at night slept in school the following day and did not have time to prepare for the next day's assignments. A ratio was worked out by the Fort Wayne school system so that the number of hours a student wanted to work were compared with the subjects he or she could take. For example, if you wanted to work up to 20 hours per week, you could take four subjects; if you wanted to work 21 to 30 hours per week you could take three subjects; 31 to 40 hours of work per week two subjects; 41 to 50 hours of work per week one subject; and over 50 hours of work per week no subjects could be taken. Some students dropped out of school to work full time in the war effort or enlisted in military service if they were of sufficient age to do so.[30]

Several South Side faculty members worked in local war industry as well as teaching. Rowena Harvey, for example, worked on the railroad.[31] In November of 1942, R. Nelson Snider was named rationing coordinator for Allen County. His job was to organize the work of the three local war price and rationing boards in controlling the distribution of all rationed articles other than tires, automobiles, typewriters, and bicycles. Perhaps the greatest contribution by South Side students toward the war effort was the purchase of stamps and savings bonds. Anyone who attended school during World War II will remem-

Many graduates descended these stairs.

Thelma Epstein and Ronnie
Altevogt relax by dancing

ber purchasing each week five cent or ten cent stamps which would be placed in a book and then redeemed for the purchase of a bond. At South Side High School during the four years of World War II, U.S Defense stamps were sold one day a week when home room periods were lengthened 15 minutes.

R. Nelson Snider appointed Pauline VanGorder to head the war effort at South Side. During the war years, Miss VanGorder organized students in the purchase of stamps and bonds and various goals were set in numerous bond drives. In center hall were charts, thermometers, grafts, etc., all indicating the progress of South Side High School in the purchase of stamps and bonds. During one period, South Side had 100% participation by all students in the purchase of stamps and bonds for 41 consecutive weeks.[32] Keith Lakey was appointed Miss VanGorder's assistant and student head of the war organization. Other students who assisted were Alvin Haley, Tom Longfellow, Albert Kranz, and the various home room war agents.[33] During World War II, South Side students purchased the amazing total of $3,293,066.55 in bonds. It should be noted that in reaching this total in a series of bond drives, the students were assisted by certain "mystery men" who matched some of the amounts raised by the students. These "mystery men" were later revealed to be prominent Fort Wayne bankers Harry Hogan, James Haberly, Charles Buesching as well as Mayor Harry Baals and the City Utilities Fund.[34] Added to more than $3 million in bond purchases, South Side students added 35,000 pounds of paper, 147 pounds of keys, 450 pounds of scrap rubber, 70 pounds of razor blades, 40 pounds of collapsible metal, 3,058 pieces of jewelry and 1,750 coat hangers.

The United States government during World War II set various incentives for schools and industry to raise money for the war effort. Various flags and emblems were presented as goals were reached. In addition, organizations collecting large amounts of money could apply specific amounts of money toward the purchase of various weapons of war such as airplanes, tanks, jeeps, etc. Early in the war, South Side High School raised $75,000 and purchased a pursuit plane which was named, "Fort Wayne's Fighting Archers."[35] As a result of raising in excess of $3 million, South Side students were able to purchase a B-24 Liberator heavy bomber, a B-25 Mitchell medium bomber, a jeep, a light tank, an armed reconnaissance car, a barrage balloon, an ambulance, two Army mules and once month's feed for a carrier pigeon.[36] Students of South Side also established a war shrine which was installed in the upper hall. Servicemen on leave could register their names at the shrine and the names of each South Side student who was a member of the armed forces were placed on separate bars in the shrine.[37]

Under the direction of Pauline VanGorder, the fighting spirit of South Side was organized. Serving on the faculty committee were Rowena Harvey, chairman, Blanche Hutto, in charge of art work, and Emma Kiefer, who saw to it that an average of 1,200 letters were mailed to all ex-archers serving in

1944 FOOTBALL TEAM – RECORD 8-1

First row, left to right: Don Chalmers, Tom Selecter, Karl Wuttke, Jack Reed, Dick Paul, Willis Disler, Don Schoenherr, Jim Kilpatrick, Ray Rolf, Dick Beery, Dick McMahon, Jim Stambaugh.

Second row: Jim Stern, Dick Snouffer, Don Wright, Bill Gale, Gene Holtrey, David Double, Keith Miller, Bob McClain, Bill Hoover, Dick Ellenwood, Herb Gernand, Joe Fields.

Third row: Don Campbell, Carl Jones, Willis Allmandinger, Jack Federspiel, Jim Hettler, Don Giese, Larry Jenney, Bob Richards, Tom Watson, Dave Erwin, Joe James, Bob Minier, Dan Ferber, Paul Snyder.

Fourth row:Assistant Coach Wayne Scott, Ned Buschman, Dick Van Curen, Dick Gottschal, Don Jung, Bob Lyman, Bob Fuzzy,Gene Snouffer, Charles Scheele, Bob Rohyans, Vorn Peterson, Don Perrine, Jim Hostetter, Coach George Collyer.

the armed forces. Also serving were Lucy Osborne who organized all of the assembly programs, C. A. Bex, who was responsible for construction work, Lester Hostetler, who was in charge of music, and Earl Murch who had the substantial job of filling orders for stamps and bonds. Not to be outdone by the faculty, the students organized a war council. Under the direction of officers and council members plus 20 homeroom representatives, the students did their part. Every Wednesday morning, without fail, there was a short program over the PA system. On Thursdays, the fruits of Wednesday's labors were announced. The assemblies that were held were actually bond rallies. Pauline VanGorder, director of South Side's war activities, remembered proudly her contributions and leadership during World War II. When interviewed by this writer, she related a most interesting incident. For each particular bond drive, a financial goal would be set. The entire school would work toward achieving that monetary goal so that they could buy a piece of military equipment such as a plane or jeep. As the war years went on, the goals became increasingly more difficult to meet. After finishing one particular bond drive, Miss VanGorder announced to her home room that the school had done a fine job but that they had fallen short of their goal. After making this announcement, the bell rang and the students left to go to their first period class. Remaining in the room was one student who approached Miss VanGorder's desk and asked the question, "How short were we?" Miss VanGorder confided to the boy that, "We were about $75,000 short." The boy said, "Don't worry, I'll have a check for you tomorrow." Miss VanGorder was somewhat astonished the next day when the boy brought in a $75,000 check from his grandfather, thus allowing South Side to meet its goal. Miss VanGorder declined to reveal the identities of either the student or his benevolent grandfather.[38]

Even though the war was the number one priority in everyone's life for nearly four years, normal events did take place on the "home front." Likewise, activities at South Side High School progressed somewhat as they had in the past despite World War II. Ruth Werkman was chosen Ivy Queen for 1942.[39] The Meterite Club, the little sister of Philo, had a very active year in 1942. The advisor was Miss Susen Peck, who had become sponsor of the club when she arrived at South Side in 1927.[40] Coach Burl Friddle's final South Side basketball team posted 16 victories but lost to Central in the 1942 sectional championship. Burl Friddle left South Side in 1942 to accept the head coaching position at the University of

Archers Celebrate Silver Anniversary

Climaxing our twenty-fifth anniversary was this colorful and unusual assembly in which over 300 Kellys participated. The theme of the entire program was taken from the plaque on the northeast corner of the school, which tells the purpose and real object of education. Mrs. Rieke narrated the program, which was divided into three parts. A public performance was given in the evening.

Upper left: Some of our Kelly teachers in their black satin robes. Upper right: Graduates in the armed forces return to strike the note of dignity, for they served in the war that youth might keep the way of life. Lower left: "The real object of education-occupation" is explained by these grads. Lower right: Here a group of sophomores tell us about South Side. "The real object of education–habits and resources" was the theme.

Toledo. By 1942, many of the Archer students were children of parents who had also graduated from South Side.[41] The 1942 graduating class, South Side's first war-time class consisted of 435 students and was the largest in school history.[42] As school opened in September of 1942, two notable additions to the faculty were Mary Graham and Wayne Scott. Mary Graham was a graduate of the South Side class of 1929 and was to remain on the South Side staff as a teacher and guidance counselor for more than 30 years. Likewise, Wayne Scott, who succeeded Burl Friddle as basketball coach and would later become athletic director, remained at South Side for more than three decades.

Following the enlistment of football coach Wayne Gift in the United States Navy, the Archer grid teams were coached during the war years by George Collyer. Coach Collyer's 1944 Archer football team had one of the best records in school history winning eight games and losing only one. Among the outstanding football players during the war years were Harry Hines, Vic Moeller, Walt Gilbert, and Ward Gilbert, Jr., (sons of former coach Ward Gilbert), Robert Gernand, who was later to become South Side's highly successful football coach, Dick Berry, Dick Ellenwood, Dick Papai, Willis Disler, Paul Snider, Bill Hoover, Tommy Selecter, Dick Schoenherr, Danny Ferber, Dick Paul, Dick McMahon, Carl Wuttke, Gene Holtrey, Ray Rolf, Joe Fields, Keith Miller and Bob McClain. The Archer basketball teams posted winning records but in 1943, 1944 and 1945, they lost to Central in the sectional tournament. The 1942-43 Archer basketball team, the first under Wayne Scott, was the only team to defeat the eventual

Hail to the Quarter Centurions: Sixteen teachers have been with the faculty since South Side opened its doors They are, front row, left to right: Miss Adelaide Fiedler, head of the mathematics department; Miss Mabel Thorne, mathematics; Miss Beulah Rinehart, English; Miss Elizabeth Demaree, English; Miss Crissie Mott, home economics; Miss Hazel Miller, social science. Back row: Louie Hull, physics; Benjamin Null, head of the English department; Maurice Murphy, head of the social science department; Elna Gould, botany and biology; Ward Gilbert, head of the science department; Earl Murch, head of the commercial department; Lloyd Whelan, physical geography; Miss Rowena Harvey, director of publications; Delivan Parks, commerce, and Miss Martha Pittenger, dean.

state champion Central Tigers during the regular season. The standout Archer basketball players during this period were Eugene "Jeep" Haynes, Luke Majorki, Al Leaky, Bob Senseny, and Bob Ruckel.[43] At the 1942 state track meet, Dick Kilpatrick won first place in the high jump, and at the 1944 state track meet, Bill Stultz won first place in the high hurdles. Ralph Shimer set a long-standing school record in the 220 yard dash in 1942, and on the 1944 track team, Tom Rehrer won numerous victories in the mile and 880, making him one of the state's best distance men.[44]

During the war years, South Side students continued to distinguish themselves in various academic areas. In the 1943 state Latin contest, Victor Kaufman and Sally Muller were first place winners.[45] These years were banner years for the South Side speech and dramatics department under the direction of Dorothy Benner Rieke. In 1943, Harvey Cocks, Jr., won the state speech contest in original oratory. John Olcott was state radio champion, John Verts was state rotary discussion champion and Robert Zimmer won the state extemporaneous championship for the second year in a row. Other state champions in 1943 in speech were Franklin Neff, Fred Collins and Jerry Mansbach.[46] The following year at the state speech meet, South Side continued its domination when Jerry Miller won first place in dramatic declamation, Al Moellering won first place in humorous declamation and Phil Traycoff won first place in radio broadcasting.[47] At the 1944 Recognition Day ceremonies, Bob Haller received the "Quiz Kid" award from R. Nelson Snider for being chosen from a city-wide competition to participate in the "Quiz Kid" radio program when it appeared in Fort Wayne.[48] In the vocal music department, Lester Hostetler continued to build a quality program during the war years. He founded a new choir called the Vesper Choir, which during the 1943-44 school year made 65 appearances.[49] The outstanding soloists of the South Side Choir during this period were Phil Steigerwald and Marion Stults.[50] In the instrumental music department, Jack Wainwright departed in 1943 and was replaced by Richard Guthier who in turn was replaced by Herbert Arlington.[51] In May of 1945, Eric Baade won first place in the State Latin Contest.[52]

Despite the best efforts of teachers and students, normal school activities could not escape the influence of World War II. The theme of the junior banquet of the class of 1943, which was held in 1942, was "Junior Draft."[53] The class of 1945 held its junior banquet in November of 1943, and the theme was "Swing Shift." Signs with slogans such as "If You're Absent You're Helping the Axis," or "No Smoking Please" were distributed around the room. Programs were cut into the design of lunch boxes and were dis-

1949 – LESTER HOSTETLER AND CHOIR

tributed with identification badges. Alvin Haley, who acted as toast master, wore a factory cap and goggles. At the close of each speech, he blew a large factory whistle to bring the students to order.[54] By the end of World War II, 18 and 19 year old boys were being drafted into the Army. In the class of 1945, there were 28 boys who were drafted into the Army before they were able to finish their senior year at South Side.[55] In the closing days of World War II, South Side celebrated its tenth Ivy Day as Coleen Albersmeyer was crowned as Ivy Day Queen for 1945. George McClain, the six-year old son of mathematics teacher Ralph McClain, later to become salutatorian of the graduating class of 1956, was the crown bearer at the tenth Ivy Day ceremonies.[56]

B. 25 Candles on the Cake

As World War II ended, South Side High School and the rest of the country attempted to return to normal activities. Joining the South Side faculty in September of 1945 was Marion Feasel, who was to served for several years as head football coach. Ernest Walker and Francis Fay rejoined the faculty, having completed their military service. Mabel Thorne's homeroom 52 adopted a young British war orphan. The Junior Town Meeting participants were Bob Haller, Keith Murphy, Lee Woods, Cynthia Koerber, Tom Watson, Hugh Arnold, Lou Ann Kayser, Don Sibley, Sheldon Stern, Jacky Sterner, Louis Bloom and Don Bitsberger.[57] In December of 1945, Jacky Sterner was selected as the recipient of the "Good Citizen Award" given by the Daughters of the American Revolution.[58] In June of 1946, Dorothy Benner Riecke retired after serving 17 years on the South Side faculty during which time she produced some of South Side's finest public speakers.[59] In September of 1946, John W. Broom became the new director of the South Side band.[60] In November of 1946, 400 people attended Philo's 25th annual after game dance known as the "Touchdown Twirl."[61]

During this early post World War II period, Coach Wayne Scott developed some of the finest basketball teams to ever represent South Side High School. In the first three post-war basketball seasons, the Archers lost only six regularly scheduled games. Unfortunately, this was the same period in which many other city schools had outstanding basketball teams. The Central Tigers went all the way to the final game of the 1946 state high school basketball tournament. During these first three post-war seasons, Coach Scott's teams managed to win only one sectional and one regional. In 1947, they advanced to the Muncie Super Regional and were defeated by Marion. The 1946-47 team lost only one game during the regular season. From 1945 until 1949, South Side won an incredible 37 consecutive games on its home floor.[62] Included among the standout basketball players during this three-year period were Bill Bower, John Bragg, Norman Greiner, Bob Garrison, Kenton Gidley, Gordon Stauffer, Gerald Goodwin, Phil McClure, Dick Berry, Bill Berry, Bob "Bo" Mossman, Bob Nye, Keith Clauser, Don Rodenbeck, Doug Lawrence, Paul Underwood, Fritz Schultz, Chuck Scheele, Louie Waters, and Willie Russell. Willie Russell was the leading scorer of the outstanding 1946-47 team and was the first of South Side's many great African American athletes.[63]

The outstanding event of the post-World War II period at South Side High School was the celebration of the school's 25th anniversary which took place on May 28, 1947. Two programs were held to commemorate the silver anniversary. There was an 8:30 a.m., program held in the gymnasium for students and at 8 p.m., there was a second program for the general public. The executive chairman of the 25th anniversary celebration was R. Nelson Snider and the general chairman was Lucy Osborne.[64] During the first 25 years of South Side High School, there had been more than 40,000 students enrolled in the school.[65] The highlight of the 25th anniversary celebration was the induction of the first class of faculty members into the Quarter Century Club. In 1947, there were 16 teachers on the South Side faculty who were present when South Side first opened its doors in 1922. These 16 teachers were as follows: Adelaide Feidler, head of the Mathematics Department, Mabel Thorne, Beulah Rinehart, English teacher, Elizabeth Demaree, English teacher, Crissie Mott, Home Economics teacher, Hazel Miller, Social Science teacher, Louie Hull, Physics, Benjamin Null, head of the English Department and author of the famous book called, "The English Sentence," Maurice Murphy, head of the Social Science Department, Elna Gould, Botany teacher, Ward Gilbert, head of the Science Department, Earl Murch, head of the Commercial Department, Lloyd Whelan, Physical Geography teacher, Rowena Harvey, Director of Publications, Delivan Parks, Commerce teacher and Martha Pittenger, Dean.[66]

In the mid to late 1940's, South Side continued to produce speech and dramatics winners. Among those excelling in this category were Don Bitsburger, Jim Solomon, Joe Christoff, Ruth Makey, Duncan Whitaker, Pat Close, Bob Johnson, Louis Bloom, Ray Epperson and Joan Ludwig.[67] During this same period, South Side continued to field excellent athletic teams. Coach George Collyer produced some of South Side's greatest track and cross teams in the late 1940's. The 1947 track team was undefeated in dual meets and finished second in the sectional. The standouts on this team were John LaBrash, Ed Roth, Bob Johnson, Ted Thieme and Bill Berry. In 1947 Bob Johnson became the first Archer to win the state cross country championship. The 1948 cross country team went undefeated and won the sectional title.[68] The 1948 track team tied North Side for the sectional title and Bill Berry, Keith Clauser, John LaBrash, Bud Hovarter, Ted Thieme and Ed Roth all qualified for the state meet.[69] On the football field, Marion Feasel became South Side grid iron coach in 1947, and his team won the city championship with such outstanding players as Marshall Warshauer, Bob Mumma, Bill Kempf, Marvin Ramage, Bill Schultz and Ed Roth.[70] Ed Roth was one of South Side's truly great football players and later went on to star at Indiana University as well as playing professional football in both the United States and Canada. The 1948 Archer football team repeated as city champions with such outstanding players as Bill Berry, Dick Brett, Doug Lawrence, Arnie Hofmann, Ev Tunget, Norm Fryback, Tom Lebamoff, Dick Eitman, Dick Wert, Paul Underwood, Jerry Ellenwood and Stan Wickliffe.[71]

In the late 1940's, South Side High School continued to be guided by two individuals who had been present since the 1920's, namely Principal R. Nelson Snider and Dean of Girls Martha Pittenger (the aunt of Lucy Osborne). Paul Sidell, veteran math teacher, became guidance director.[72] Notable additions to the faculty in the late 1940's included Robert Drummond and Glen Stebing, who joined the faculty in 1947, and Robert Weber, who joined the faculty in 1948. Mr. Drummond became the band director and for many years was golf coach. Mr. Stebing came to South Side to teach a brand new subject, driver training, and in 1948 succeeded Wayne Scott as head basketball coach. He would later become director of South Side's intramural program. Mr. Weber replaced South Side's original botany teacher, Elna Gould, and became one of South Side's most popular teachers serving for many years as advisor of the Hi-Y Club. Mr. Drummond, Mr. Stebing, and Mr. Weber were each to remain at South Side for more than 35 years.

In the spring of 1948, Archer students were invited to drop into Room 170 every day from 12:45 p.m. to 1:20 p.m. The students were invited to bring their own records, and the school bought a new phonograph on which to play the records for noon time dancing. In March of 1948, it was announced that the annual GAA spring show was to have a Mexican fiesta theme. Helen Pohlmeyer and Alice Keegan were to direct 500 girls who would participate in this pageant.[73] Phyllis Miller received the high point award from GAA in the spring of 1948, while John Birk became the first boy in the history of South Side to win four intramural letters.[74] In 1948, for the 25th consecutive year, the Columbia Scholastic Press Association presented the medalist award, its highest honor, to the *South Side Times*. The sports page, under the editorship of Stan Knapp, won the All Columbian award for being the best in the country among schools with an enrollment of 1,000 to 1,500.[75] By the late 1940's, the effect of the low birth rate during the depression years was being felt at South Side. Student enrollment which had been at or near 2,000 students during the late 1930's and most of the 1940's declined to approximately 1,500. This enrollment would decline even further in the early and middle 50's before rising again.

As the decade of the 1940's ended, certain traditions were firmly fixed in student life at South Side. In 1949, the 14th Ivy Day was celebrated with the crowning of Joella Seibert as Ivy Day Queen, and the selection of Vickie Turpchinoff, Jane Hawver, Bonnie Schemehorn and Jerry Kierspe as her attendants.[76] In December of 1949, the Chamber of Commerce speech contest was held at the Wrangler's meeting in the Greeley Room. Max Hobbs won first place and received $7.50 for his speech. Second place was won by Ruth Havens who received $6.00, while Ivan Lebamoff received $4.00 for third place and Dorothy Kelsey was given $2.50 for fourth place.[77]

1947 Ivy Day Parade

1946-47 Basketball team with 23 wins and two losses.
Left to right: Keith Clauser, Bill Bower, Phil McClure, Bob Nye, Gordie Stauffer, Gerald Goodwin, Bud Greiner, Bob Mossman, Fritz Schulz, Louie Water, Willie Russell and Chuck Scheele.

Let us do our work as well,
    Both the unseen and the seen;
Make the house, where Gods may dwell,
    Beautiful, entire, and clean.

CHAPTER FOUR
1950 ~ 1959

A. I Like Ike and Elvis Too

The 1950's which are remembered with fondness as extremely carefree productive years in American history were eventful at South Side High School. Fashion advice for female students indicated that hem lines were going up. Skirts were hanging 14 to 16 inches from the floor with mid calf being the ideal length. The slim skirt was definitely out of style. Belted Russian blouses were a big hit in the early winter of 1950 and middy blouses were getting just as much attention.[1] In the early winter of 1950, after 28 long years of misery, left-handed students at South Side finally received relief as special custom made desks for left-handers were delivered.[2] The songs popular at South Side in early 1950 included, "Music, Music, Music" by Teresa Brewer, "Rag Mop" with the Jimmy Dorsey Orchestra, "I Said My Pajamas and Put on My Prayers" by Doris Day and "Dear Hearts and Gentle People" by Bing Crosby.[3] Archers who wanted to dance to the music of Woody Neff and his orchestra at the Prom Terrace could take the free bus service which left from the transfer corner on Sunday afternoons at 2 p.m., and returned immediately after the dance.[4]

In the 1950's, the faculty tradition of the "Boiler Room Dinner" was going strong. Paul Sidell, long-time South Side faculty member, remembers the boiler room with great fondness. It was located in the basement and became a hangout for a certain group of male faculty members who gathered there to eat lunch and play cards. The male teachers were allowed to smoke in the boiler room and could relax in this informal atmosphere. According to Mr. Sidell, there were certain teachers who went to the boiler room and certain other teachers who went to either the mens' faculty lounge or the womens' faculty lounge. Included among the male faculty leaders in the boiler room were Stanley Post, Earl Sterner, and Ernest Walker.[5] Each year, the female faculty members gave a Christmas luncheon for the male teachers with very fancy doilies and other decorations. Each year the faculty men would have their own rough and ready luncheon for the faculty women at which there were no doilies, no decorations of any kind and navy beans were served. George Robert Davis remembers frequenting the boiler room as a young teacher. Each noon, there was a game of Tong which was a card game similar to Poker. Occasionally, R. Nelson Snider would come to the boiler room and join in these games.[6]

The early 1950's saw significant departures and additions to the South Side faculty. Several of the 16 original faculty members retired during this period. In 1950, Martha Pittenger who had served as dean of girls since the opening of South Side, retired. She was replaced by Pauline VanGorder.[7]

1953 — Mr. John Edgebert, of Caprehart-Farnsworth, demonstrates a television set to Math-Science. (No television was available for this meeting. The picture was "dubbed" in.)

1949 - Darrell Blanton receives a first day welcome from the seniors.

Also retiring in the early 1950's were original faculty members Benjamin Null, Delivan Parks, Crissie Mott, Elizabeth Demaree, Beulah Rinehart, Maurice Murphy, Adelaide Fiedler and Louie Hull. Mary Edith Reiff, future head of the Foreign Language Department and long-time Latin teacher, joined the faculty in 1950.[8] During the 1951-52 school year, there were significant faculty reassignments as well as new teachers joining the staff. Ora Davis, long-time athletic director, became guidance director. Paul Sidell, who had been guidance director, replaced Adelaide Fiedler as head of the Math Department. In September of 1951, Wilburn Wilson became head of the Social Studies Department replacing Maurice Murphy who had retired. Notable additions to the faculty in September of 1951 were Robert Petty, long-time Math teacher who replaced Adelaide Fiedler and Don Reichert, a for-

mer South Side student who became basketball coach and would guide the Archer teams to more victories than any basketball coach in South Side history. Also joining the South Side faculty in the autumn of 1951 was Jack Weicker who replaced Maurice Murphy in the Social Studies Department. Mr. Weicker, of course, became principal of South Side High School in 1963.[9] Other new teachers arriving in the fall of 1951 included William Applegate, Marvey Knigge, Shirley Maloney and Jack Morey. Additional original faculty members or long-time faculty members retiring in the early 1950's included Herman Makey, Mabel Thorne, Mary McCloskey, Emma Kiefer and GeorgeAnna Hodgson. A sad event occurred in June of 1952 when Louis Briner, intramural director since 1929, died unexpectedly. He was replaced by Clair Motz, former head basketball coach at North Side High School who remained on the South Side faculty for many years and did an outstanding job as Mr. Briner's successor in the intramural program.[10] Additional teachers joining the South Side staff in the early 1950's included Evlyn Spray, Mildred Luse and David Cramer.

On the national scene, South Korea was invaded by North Korea in June of 1950 and for the next three years the Korean War would more or less dominate national headlines. In 1952, World War II hero Dwight Eisenhower was elected president and would serve as a benevolent father figure in the White House for the remainder of the 1950's. In the early 1950's, both boys and girls at South Side were wearing saddle shoes. Archer students still attended pep sessions, sat freshmen on the fountain, and went to football games, basketball games and after-game dances. The "hangouts" for South Side students in the early 1950's were Miller's, Zoob's Place (directly across the street from South Side High School on the hill), and the South Side Grill.[11] The South Side Times. still under the direction of original faculty member Rowena Harvey, continued to gather honors in the early 1950's.

On the basketball court, the Archer netters coached by Glen Stebing won the city championship in 1950. This excellent team which unfortunately lost by one point to Central in the sectional tournament featured such outstanding players as Merle Hettler, Gene Towns, Norm Fryback, Jerry Ellenwood,

Alex Tsiguloff, Tom Skole and Jack Miller.[12] The Archer football teams of the early 1950's were coached by Marion Feasel who was replaced in 1953 by Jack Bobay.

Outstanding Archer football players during this period were Charles Littlejohn, Dick VanHorn, Allan Wuebbenhorst, Louis Mangels, Miles Murphy, Paul Casterline, Dan Perrey, Keith Saylor, Don Rife, Jim Craig, Mike Melchior and Jim McGraw. With the exception of the 1950 city championship team, the Archer basketball teams of the early 1950's did not post winning records but did produce some outstanding players including John Sweet, Jim Ruble, Dick Bragg, Al McClure and Darrell Blanton. Perhaps South Side's greatest success in athletics in the early 1950's came in track and field. In 1950, Ev Tunget won the state championship in the shot put. The 1951 track season was a banner year which saw Coach George Collyer's squad finish second at the state meet. Perhaps in no other track season were as many school records broken as in 1951. The 440 yard relay team composed of Bill Davis, Don Personett, James Smith and Dick VanHorn established a new record. Warren Anderson, Charles Littlejohn, Harry Clauser and Allan Wuebbenhorst broke the mile relay record at the Marion relays. The sprint relay record was broken by the team of Barry Gemmer, Kent Horton, Charles Littlejohn and Allan Wuebbenhorst. Charles Littlejohn set a new school broad jump record while Warren Anderson set a school record in the high jump. In addition, Lee Johnson set new records in the high and low hurdles.[13] At the state track meet in 1952, Warren Anderson, one of South Side's all time great track standouts, won first place in both the high jump and low hurdles.[14] Other Archer track standouts of the early 1950's were Stanley Collyer, Keith Darby, Harley Stuntz, Jim LaBrash and Dick Brantingham.[15] By 1951, South Side's corps of all male cheerleaders had been replaced by mostly females. The 1951-52 varsity cheerleaders were Radka Gouloff, Katie Schulz, Treva Greenwalt and Nancy Kierspe. The only male cheerleader was Jim Swank.[16] In 1952, ace Archer golfer Ken Rodewald shot a 71 at the Brookwood Golf Course. This score of 71 still stands as an all-time South Side record.[17]

In 1951, R. Nelson Snider celebrated his 25th year as principal of South Side High School. At the Quarter Century Club meeting held on April 26, 1951, an oil portrait of Mr. Snider which had been painted by Mrs. Grace Leslie Dickerson was unveiled.[18] Joining Mr. Snider as members of the Quarter Century Club in 1951 were Emma Shoup, librarian, and Wilburn Wilson, head of the Social Studies Department.[19] In 1951, Mr. Snider was a leading candidate to replace Merle J. Abbett as superintendent of the Fort Wayne Schools, but the position was given to Aaron T. Lindley, and Mr. Snider was to continue for another 12 years as principal of South Side High School. In the fall of 1952, the Patterson Fletcher Department Store was selling South Side belt buckles with a bronze and silver background for $1.95.[20] Also in the fall of 1952, Betsy Waterfield was announced as the winner of the Randolph Jacobs Service Award.[21] In the early 1950's, South Side students continued to excel in various academic activities. Nancy Kierspe and Ted Gugler received first place in their respective divisions at the Ball State speech meet.[22] Students receiving recognition in the regional math contest held in March of 1953 were Charles Clarkson, Robert Noren, Janice Hattendorf, George McClain, Kenneth Clark, Mike Melchior and Don Rife.[23] In the summer of 1953, Ralph Elston and Bob Rossiter each received a silver medal for outstanding academic achievement at Culver Military Academy's summer naval course.[24] That same summer, Archer senior Phil Thieme travelled around the world, and among other adventures, was able to gain an audience with the President of Egypt.[25]

By the autumn of 1953, enrollment at South Side had fallen to 1,368. This meant that South Side was the second largest high school in town. Central was the largest high school.[26] Due to the declining enrollment which was caused by the low birth rate of the late depression years of the 1930's, only 57% of the South Side High School facility was being utilized. During the same time period, Fort Wayne's grade schools and junior highs were experiencing over crowded conditions. In January of 1954, the seventh and eighth grade students from Merle J. Abbett School were moved to South Side. Long-time South Side math teacher Ralph McClain was named principal of the junior high. This marked the first time since 1925 that grade school students had been housed at South Side.[27]

In 1954, white bucks, blue suede shoes, grey flannel trousers, Bermuda shorts, long white socks, penny loafers and flat top haircuts were in at South Side High School. Out were the musical sounds of the 1940's and early 1950's which were replaced by a more up tempo beat at first called rhythm and blues and later known as rock and roll. Waiting in the wings not as yet prominent on the national stage were such personalities as Elvis Presley and James Dean. At 3601 South Calhoun Street, the musical menu of South Side High School was being ably presented by Robert Drummond, the instrumental director, and Lester Hostetler, the choir director. At the state music contest held in Indianapolis early in 1954, Archer students Dean Dauscher, Janet Sauer, Nancy Zeiler, Ruth Pifer, Judy Cook, Marcia Downhour, Phyllis Krouse and Dale Barrett all received a superior rating.[28] Outstanding among the musical accompanists at South Side High School in the mid 50's were pianists Lou Gerig and Colleen Liddy. Speaking of pianists, who could ever forget the outstanding imitations of Liberace performed by senior Jim McGraw. At the junior banquet, the boys sextet consisting of Tom Sites, Jim Frey, Ken Scrogham, Stuart Koch, Tom Arnold and Bob Rossiter provided the entertainment.[29] Additional outstanding Archer musicians in the mid 1950's were Sue Berlien and Carl Simon whose band played at many school dances.[30] During this period, South Side was blessed with many outstanding female dancers such as Mary Val Crouse who appeared on several network television shows.[31] Other outstanding dancers of the period were Judy Hicks[32] and Susie Sigrist.[33]

The South Side Times in the mid 1950's continued to gather national honors. In the Times room presided over as always by Rowena Harvey, her ever-present dog Patsy was getting acquainted with the boiler room cat named Smokey.[34] During the summer of 1954, South Side female swimmers dominated that sport. Carolyn Morrill set a record in winning the 50 meter free style and another Archer Liz Moore placed in two events. Among the new teachers who joined the faculty in the autumn of 1954 was Robert Gernand, who would remain at South Side for more than three decades and produce some of the most successful football teams in school history.[35] Later that year, C.A. Bex, veteran industrial arts teacher, joined the Quarter Century Club. Mr. Bex started his teaching career at South Side in 1930.[36] As we now know, in the mid 1950's the space age was just around the corner. South Side achieved a jump start when a science fiction type device known as a cyclotron appeared in the school basement and was attended by

1951 – Junior Prom

1952 – Ora Davis with group of students including son, George Robert Davis.

such science buffs as Dave Sutter and Fritz Bartlett.[37] One of the most exciting club events at South Side in the mid 50's was the appearance of well-known movie actor Ronald Reagan who addressed a meeting of the South Side Hi-Y Club after being introduced by senior Bruce Snyder.[38] Another exciting social event of the period was an appearance by the musical group, "The Crew-Cuts" who appeared first at the Memorial Coliseum and later at South Side High School. "The Crew-Cuts" big hits were "ShBoom" and "Crazy About You Baby."[39] Early in 1955, physics teacher Don Weaver announced that South Side would set up its own weather forecasting station. Chuck Owen was the director, Tom Baumgartner, assistant director, Courtland Clayton, chief of instruments, and Clauda Hurley, chief of records.[40] In the mid 50's, South Side High School continued to produce outstanding and successful public speakers. Joan Nading won the high school declamation contest sponsored by the Kiwanis Club in 1955.[41] Other prominent Archer speakers of this period included Paula McConnell, winner of the voice of democracy speech contest, and Morrie Sanderson.[42]

Long-time Archer traditions were alive and well in the mid 50's. The Randolph Jacobs Service Trophy was won by MaryAnn Wilkens,[43] and in 1955 Roselyn Roof was crowned as South Side's 20th Ivy Day Queen continuing the tradition which began in 1936.[44] The senior class play presented by the class of 1955 was "Cuckoos On The Hearth" directed by Jack Morey. Cast members included Stan Lipp, Mary Val Crouse, Norma Jacobs, Tom Arnold, John Johnson, Tom Sites, Jane Zeiler, Karen Keller, Colleen Liddy and Neal Berryhill.[45] In the academic arena, Kip Riddle was awarded first prize at the Northeast Indiana Regional Science Fair[46] while Tom Doty and Jack Ford, both members of the class of 1956, received the R. Nelson Snider Latin Award.[47]

Among the new faculty members in the autumn of 1955 were three South Side graduates, LaVerne Harader, Bill Geyer and George Schlenker.[48] In the fall of 1956, new faculty members included former South Side graduate Donna Jean Roebel, Myrtle Grimshaw, Richard Bussard, who was to remain on the faculty for more than 30 years, and John Arnold, another teacher destined to be a member of the Quarter Century Club. Mr. Arnold replaced original faculty member Hazel Miller.[49]

On the athletic field, the South Side High School football teams of the mid 1950's managed few victories but did produce some outstanding individuals. The 1954 and 1955 football squads coached by Jack Bobay won only one regular season game.[50] In 1956, Robert Gernand, a South Side graduate, became football coach. In the first season under Gernand, the South Side gridders won four and lost four. Five Archers from this team, namely Jim VaChon, Chris Stavreti, John L. Clark, Rich Miller and George Bobilya were named to the All City team.[51] Other outstanding Archer football players during the mid-1950's were Norman Miner, Dennis McIntyre, Ellis Ralston, Jim Fuzy, Bob Blanton and Dave Matthias.[52]

Glen Stebing and Driver's Training

South Side's basketball program under Coach Don Reichert, "turned the corner" during the 1953-54 season as they won 16 games, while losing only four. In the sectionals, they lost by two points to a strong North Side team. Outstanding players on this Archer basketball squad were Fred Augspurger, Bill Chavis, John Adamonis, Jack Kern and Don Johnson.[53] 1954-55 was a rebuilding year for Coach Reichert, and this team produced such individual standouts as Bill Gerig, Bob Rossiter, Bob Wright, Jim Frey, Bruce Scott and Dan Howe, who made the team as a freshman.[54] The following year, the cry of "save your confederate money boys, South Side will rise again" echoed throughout Archer pep sessions and was displayed on banners at games. The words were prophetic as in 1956 South Side claim its first sectional and regional basketball titles in nine years. Players instrumental in this rejuvenation of South Side basketball were Terry Miller, Bob Blackledge, John Lewis, George Wehrmeister, Bill Campbell and John Beal.[55]

During the mid-50's, George Collyer continued to produce excellent track and cross country teams. At the 1955 North Side relays, the Archer track team upset the highly favored North Side Redskins. The two-mile relay team set a new record at this meet. Members of this team were John Sawyer, Dave Redding, Dick Lentz and Bob Wright. In addition, the Archers set a record in the half-mile relay. This team was composed of Bob Wright, Paul Dailey, Terry Miller and Wade Altevogt.[56] At the 1956 state track meet, South Side's 880 yard relay team composed of Chris Stavreti, Dan Howe, Terry Miller and Tom Pinder won the title. At the 1956 state cross country meet, Dave Redding of South Side won the individual championship running the distance in near record time to become the second Archer in history to claim this title.[57] In the mid-1950's, the female athletes of South Side High School were extremely active through their participation in the Girls Athletic Association. In 1955, Carolyn DeHaven was GAA high point girl scoring 2,530 points during her four-year career.[58] The GAA point leaders for the 1955-56 season were Nancy Showalter and Becky Brinkroeger. Among the GAA officers in 1955-56 were Luba Gouloff, Carol Oyer, Sharon Sprunger and Sandra Howser. Outstanding intramural athletes included Russ Oyer, Herb Stuelpe and Bill Chapman.[59] From 1953 to 1955, the tennis team under Everett Havens scored 25 consecutive wins and won the city championship in 1953, 1954, and 1955. Archer tennis standouts during this period were Dave Stratton, Dave Gustafson, Dick Colchin, Lowell Zoller, Jerry O'Brien, Dave Benhoff, Dick Cashman, Bill Gerig, LaMont Hansen and Jim Miller.[60] The resurgence of South Side athletics during the mid 1950's was reported to Archer readers by such outstanding sports journalists as Stan Levine, Phil Sosinski, Mary Brunskill and Chris Litchin.[61]

B. State Champs Again

In 1957, the Russians launched Sputnik and the world officially entered the "space age." At the Hi-Y dance, Ted Despos handed to Dorothy Markoff the scepter which designated her as the official "Queen of Hearts."[62] "Our Town" was presented by the class of 1957 as the senior play. The play was directed by Jack Morey, and prominent cast members included Klem Lebamoff, Judy Clark, Jim Clauser, Pam Manth, Joe Winder, Carolyn Beardsley and Terry Eads.[63] By this time, rock and roll music had taken both the country and South Side High School by storm, but there was still time for some smooth and sedate music such as that produced by the senior boys quartet made up of Ned Byrer, Joe Winder, Jim Clauser and Paul Campbell. In 1957, Bill Berg, one of the all-time great Archer golfers, shot a 72 at the Coffin Course in Indianapolis. This score was one stroke off of the school record.[64] Among those joining the faculty in the autumn of 1957 were Lowell Coats, Ronald Gersmehl, future head of the English Department, Warren Hoover, Fred Hellman and Robert Storey, who assumed sponsorship of Wrangler's and coached the speech team. Also joining the faculty at this time was George Robert Davis, a 1952 graduate of South Side High School. George and his father, Ora Davis, were the only father-son teaching team in South Side High School history. George Robert Davis would remain on the South Side faculty for 39 years until his retirement in 1996. He and his father would teach together until the retirement of Ora Davis in June of 1964.[65]

The dominant event of the late 1950's was South Side's second state championship basketball title which was won by the 1958 team. Coach Don Reichert's successful building of a strong basketball program continued in the mid and late 1950's and was, of course, climaxed by winning the 1958 state championship. Credit should be given to Coach Reichert for the overall strength and dominance of the Archer basketball program in the mid and late 1950's. From 1955 to 1960, South Side basketball teams won 34 consecutive city series games which is a Fort Wayne record.[66] Coach Reichert's 1956-1957 South Side basketball team for a second consecutive year won the city championship, sectional championship and the regional crown. They were defeated in the semi-state tournament by eventual state champion South Bend Central.[67] Outstanding players on this 1956-57 basketball team included Chris Stavreti, Ned Byrer, John L. Clark, Dave Matthias and Kip Ormerod. In addition to these senior stalwarts, names that fans statewide would be hearing in the future such as Dan Howe, Rich Miller, Carl Stavreti, Mike McCoy and Tom Bolyard were members of this team.[68] With a veteran team returning for the 1957-58 season, the expectations of Archer fans were high. These expectations were realized as the 1957-58 team lost only two games and dominated most of the teams that they played both in the city and in statewide competition. Actually, the 1957-58 team, destined to be state cham-

1956 Cross Country State Champion Dave Redding.

1958 State

Champions

pions, lost only one regularly scheduled game, an overtime defeat by Michigan City. The other loss was to Muncie Central by a margin of three points in the holiday tournament.[69] The stiffest challenge for the title bound Archers came in the semi-final of the sectional as they eked out a four-point victory over a strong Central Tiger team. The Archers breezed through the regional posting lopsided wins over Fremont and Berne, and the next week in the semi-state posted strong victories over Bluffton and Elkhart to propel them to the state finals for the fifth time in school history. (Two of these state final appearances were in the 1920's when 16-teams went to the finals.)[70]

At the 1958 state finals, the Archers who had finished the season ranked number one in the state were a qualified favorite to win the championship. The qualification was due to the presence of the Muncie Central Bearcats, one of only two teams who had defeated South Side. While the Archers were looking forward to a rematch, this was not to take place as Muncie was upset in one of the afternoon games by Crawfordsville while South Side posted a hard fought 13 point victory over a previously unde-feated Springs Valley team to advance to the final game of the state tournament for the second time in school history. In the final game of the state tournament played before a sell-out crowd of 15,000 plus fans at Butler Field House, the score was tied at the end of the first quarter 12-12. By half time, the Archers led 16-10. The "Green and White Machine" really poured it on in the second half outscoring Crawfordsville 35-12 to post a 63-34 victory, one of the widest margins of victory ever in the champi-onship game. The state champion Archers were led in scoring by Mike McCoy who scored 24 points, while Dan Howe tallied 13 points, Carl Stavreti had 12 points and Tom Bolyard scored 9 points.[71] Just before his jubilant players threw him into an icy shower, Coach Don Reichert stated, "This is the happi-est moment of my life, and I couldn't be prouder of these boys than I am right now."[72]

The celebration following the Archers victory in the 1958 state title game was equal to that of 1938 and in some ways it surpassed it. A crowd of 20,000 people gathered at Baer Field to welcome the team home on Sunday. There was a celebration at South Gate Plaza and a dinner for the team at PanDee's Restaurant.[73] The celebration actually started the night before with a record hop at the Sears parking lot. On Monday morning, the school had a pep session which was described as the "peppiest" in school his-tory. In the afternoon, there was a record hop at the Coliseum, and all of the city high schools were dis-missed.[74] The starting five of the 1958 state championship team was comprised of Dan Howe and Tom Bolyard at forwards, Mike McCoy at center and Carl Stavreti and Rich Miller at guards. Other members of the team were Larry Miller, Mike Simmons, Ken Howe, Nick DeMetre, Ted Lebrecht, Jim VaChon and Bill Meyer.[75] Following the successful 1958 state championship season, Mike McCoy was named Indiana Mr. Basketball. Carl Stavreti joined McCoy for the Indiana-Kentucky All Star game.[76] In addition, to an extremely successful basketball season, South Side's 1958 track team, coached by George Collyer, won the sectional title and tied for the regional championship. At the state track meet in 1958, Dan Howe won the low hurdles championship. Other outstanding members of this Archer track team were Rich Miller, Carl Stavreti, Dick Miller, Phil Cartwright, Ed Hartman, Mel Smith and Joe Roth.[77]

C. More Construction...But Still No Auditorium

As the decade of the 50's neared its end, new faculty members in the autumn of 1958 included Ann Arber, Florence Emshwiller, Charles P. "Porky" Holt, Ann Redmond and Richard Sage, who would remain on the South Side faculty for many years and become head of the Math Department.[78] On the

1958 State Basketball Champions. In picture at left are (left to right):
Top Row: Rich Miller, Mike McCoy, Mike Simmons, Jim VaChon, Bill Meyer, Nick DeMetre and Larry Miller.
Front Row (kneeling): Carl Stavreti, Tom Bolyard, Dan Howe and Coach Don Reichert.

Archer gridiron in the late 1950's, Coach Robert Gernand was still in the process of rebuilding the program which would bloom in the mid 1960's with some of the greatest football teams ever seen at South Side High School. The Archer football teams of the late 1950's struggled to play .500 ball. Outstanding Archer gridders in the late 1950's included Bill Meyer, Dick Tipton, Steve Gaskill, Jim Olinske, Jim Dawson and Ken Howe. The old lights in South Side stadium were replaced in the fall of 1959 and new lights were used for the first time in Archer's game against Hammond Morton on September 25, 1959. This game was won by South Side 14-6.[79] These new lights replaced the original lights installed by Central High School some 20 years previous and paved the way for South Side to join the rest of the football world in playing home games on Friday night. Thus ended the era of Saturday afternoon football at South Side Stadium. The late 50's also saw some coaching changes. Warren Hoover replaced Robert Drummond as golf coach, Robert Gernand replaced George Collyer as track coach, while Charles "Porky" Holt took over for Mr. Collyer as cross country coach."[80]

The 1958-59 basketball season was the final year of an incredible four-year cycle of championship teams assembled by Coach Don Reichert. The 1958-59 basketball team, again, defeated all the city schools both in the regular season and in the tournament. This 1958-59 basketball team proved to be a big surprise to everyone. Most of the starters from the state championship team had departed but the 1958-59 team managed to win 22 games while only losing four. The regular season included two overtime victories over arch rival Central. The 1958-59 season saw the Archers for the fourth time in a row winning the city sectional and regional titles. In the afternoon game of the 1959 semi-state, the Archers were defeated 92-90 in one of the most exciting games ever played at that level. A last-second shot by famous Kokomo player Jimmy Rayl caused the Archer defeat. The undisputed individual standout on the 1958-59 basketball team was Tom Bolyard, the only starter who returned from the state championship team. During an amazing season, Bolyard set a school career scoring record of 1,420 points. He also set a single season record of 803 points and a one game South Side record of an incredible 48 points.[81] Tom Bolyard became the first South Side basketball player to score more than 1,000 points during his high school career. In addition to Bolyard, Nick Demetre and Dave Barrett were named to the All-City team. One of South Side's future star athletes Acie Eldridge was a sophomore in this 1958-59 team. In the late 1950's, South Side continued to produce track standouts such as Ken Howe and Win Moses in the hurdles, Tom Bolyard in the half mile, and Joe Roth and Bob Shine in the quarter mile.

In January of 1959, the most significant construction project at South Side High School since the addition of the second floor in 1938 was completed. In this construction project, the original structure

1954 – Ronald Reagan, later to become President, speaks to the boys at a Hi-Y meeting. It must have been interesting because several of the members are craning their necks to see.

Robert Drummond

was extended to the east eliminating Clinton Court which was vacated between Oakdale and Darrow Avenues.[82] The homes which were constructed in the early 1940's on the east side of Clinton Court were moved to South Calhoun Street near Tillman where they stand today. On January 25, 1959, the new addition was dedicated and it included a new cafeteria and kitchen complex, a new girl's gymnasium and sports rooms, as well as remodeling of the manual training area. This construction allowed South Side to move the cafeteria from its original location on the second floor above the north entrance. At the dedication, which took place on January 25, 1959, the acceptance address was given by Superintendent of Schools Aaron T. Lindley and the South Side Choir provided the music and sang a special dedicatory song entitled, "Bless This House."[83] The end of the 1950's also marked the conclusion of South Side's final

link with the opening of the school in 1922. In 1959, the final four remaining original faculty members retired. Those final original faculty members retiring in the spring of 1959 were Rowena Harvey, long-time publications advisor, Ward Gilbert, former coach, athletic director and Science Department head, Earl Murch, head of the Commercial Department and Lloyd Whelan, long-time physical geography teacher and scorer par excellence at hundreds of South Side athletic events. In addition, Susen Peck, Jake McClure, Albert T. Heine and Lucy Mellen[84], each of whom had more than 30 years experience on the South Side faculty, retired in June of 1959.

When school opened in the autumn of 1959, there were many new faces on the faculty. Most notable among the new arrivals were Richard Block, who would later become assistant principal, and Pres Brown, later to become athletic director. Both Mr. Block and Mr. Brown would remain at South Side for more than 30 years. Another new faculty member arriving in 1959 was James Rohrabaugh who replaced Rowena Harvey as director of publications.[85] As the 1950's ended, South Side continued to hold its graduation ceremonies in the gymnasium since there was no auditorium. Those South Siders who graduated at any time from the 1920's through the early 1960's will remember how the gym was set up for graduation ceremonies. The graduating seniors came into the gym and were seated in wooden chairs on the gymnasium floor. The spectators sat in the permanent gymnasium seats. A large stage was built across the south end of the gymnasium. When the time came for the seniors to receive their diplomas, they left their seats on the gym floor and were led to the incline outside the upper south doors of the gymnasium. The seniors would then enter through the upper door, descend on some specially built stairs and then cross the stage where R. Nelson Snider would present the diploma and shake hands with each senior. After receiving the diploma and the hand shake from Mr. Snider, the biggest challenge in everyone's career at South Side High School came when they had to navigate a very steep set of stairs leading back to the gymnasium floor. The class of 1959 was one of the last to graduate in the South Side gymnasium. In the early 60's, graduation ceremonies were moved to Memorial Coliseum.

1956 – Nancy Showalter and Bill Campbell.

1957 – Varsity cheerleaders are, front row, John Henricksen, Donna Ornas, Jim Clauser; back row, Diana Goodin, Mary Johns and Ginny Shopoff.

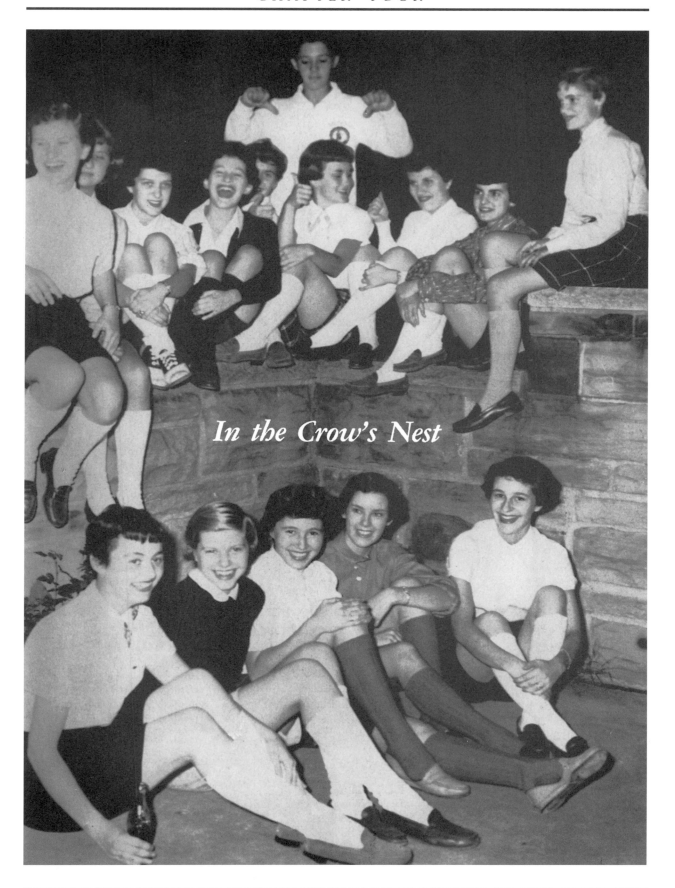

In the Crow's Nest

CHAPTER FIVE
1960-1969
A. Time Does Not Stand Still

As the 1960's began, South Side High School started its fifth decade of service to the citizens of Fort Wayne. This decade would see some of the most significant changes and notable accomplishments since South Side High School first opened its doors in 1922. The decade would begin with a spirited contest for the presidency of the United States waged for the first time by two candidates, Richard Nixon and John F. Kennedy, both born in the twentieth century. We would experience the assassination of a young president, and the United States would embark upon yet another foreign military adventure in Vietnam. This would lead the young people of the country to protest and to question the authority of the government. As the decade neared its end, we would send a man to the moon and return him safely. As times began to change, so did the educational mission of South Side High School. This is evidenced by the existence of certain clubs in the early 1960's. The Math-Science Club was succeeded by the Junior Academy of Science, Thirty-Six Workshop was replaced by the Assembly Workshop, and the Masque and Gavel Club was instituted to give special training to students interested in dramatics. Also included in the new clubs in 1960 was the Designers Associated Club sponsored by Thomas Polite. This group functioned primarily to study and work on the designing of automobiles and houses, as well as general drafting. While the 1960's ushered in a era of new clubs with new purposes and objectives, many of the old club traditions continued. "Know Your City" Club was still under the direction of Jack Weicker, assisted by Richard Block. Philo, one of South Side's oldest clubs, was under the direction of Evlyn Spray, while its little sister, the Meterites, were led by Florence Emshwiller. Hi-Y was still a very active club under the direction of Robert Weber. Ruth Fleck sponsored the Art Club, while Wranglers was under the leadership of Robert Storey. The *South Side Times*, under the direction of new advisor James Rohrabaugh, again took top honors in various national and state contests. Included among the members of the circulation staff of the *South Side Times* in 1960 was a young sophomore named Jennifer Manth, who would become principal of South Side High School.[1]

On the basketball court, Coach Don Reichert who had guided South Side to unparalleled heights in the mid to late 1950's faced the inevitable "rebuilding year." In 1960, South Side's 34 game consecutive winning streak over other city schools came to an end when the Archers were defeated by the Central Tigers. For the first time since 1955, South Side did not win the sectional basketball tournament as they bowed to Central in their first sectional game. The Central Tigers went to the state finals in 1960 for the last time in that school's history.[2] The Archer basketball team, however, would bounce back in 1961 to win South Side's fifth sectional title in six years. This team, which was eliminated in the regionals, included

Rowena Harvey and new Thunderbird

Wayne Scott

Wilburn Wilson   Mary Crowe   Ora Davis

Steve Hargan who would become an outstanding major league baseball pitcher for the Cleveland Indians and several other big league teams. The 1960 Archer football team experienced their first winning season in seven years, winning five, losing three and tieing one. Among the standout players on this team were Bob Bolyard, Bob Griffith, Chris Parrott, Jim Dawson and Bob Shine. On the cinder track in 1961, Karl Bandemer set a school record by running the 100 yard dash in 9.9 seconds while Carl Johnson won the high hurdles at the state track meet in 1961.[3]

The 1960-61 school year saw the introduction of a brand-new literary publication at South Side and the rebirth of an old publication. *Pegasus*, the Archer literary magazine, made its debut under the editorship of Bob Steiner and it went on sale in the spring of 1961 under the direction of Stan Redding, circulation manager of the *Times*. At the same time, the *Green Book*, edited by Ellen McCarron, made its first appearance in twenty years. The managing editor of the *Times* in 1961 was Sandy Thorn.[4] She would later achieve notoriety as a featured columnist for the Fort Wayne *Journal Gazette*. Included among the varsity cheerleaders and a graduate of the class of 1961 was Betty Jean Carroll, known in her South Side days as "Jeannie Carroll."[5] She would later gain nationwide fame as an author and host of an NBC television talk show using the name E. Jean Carroll. As South Side High School celebrated its thirtieth anniversary in 1962, the *Totem* for the first time increased in size to the dimensions known today. This was among several changes instituted in the post-Rowena Harvey era by James Rohrabaugh, director of publications. The size of the 1962 Totem was described as being "college size" and its editor-in chief was Babette Jones. The Archer literary publication, *Pegasus*, in its second year featured Jennifer Manth as editor-in-chief.[6] In 1962, the dance craze called the "twist" was sweeping the nation, and at the "Letterman's Twist," president Mark Hagerman crowned Nate Norment as King Kelly. By 1962, enrollment at South Side High School once again approached the 2,000 level. In the early 1960's, Coach Robert Gernand was beginning to turn around the Archer football program and winning teams began to appear. On the basketball court, Don Reichert was entering his second decade as Archer basketball mentor. In addition to serving as head football coach, Robert Gernand continued to serve as track coach in the early 1960's. Outstanding Archer football players in the early 1960's included John Weaver, Tom McMahan, Chuck Parker, Mark Hagerman, Nate Norment, Bob Lohman, Bill Cupp and Bill Rastetter. Among the outstanding basketball players of this period were Steve Hargan, Acie Eldridge, Gary Probst, and Willie Files. Notable track performers in addition to those previously mentioned were Dave Blanton and Sid Sheray.

As school opened in September of 1962, there was something conspicuously absent at South Side High School. This was the first year in the history of the school that

Pauline VanGorder

Jack Weicker and R. Nelson Snider prepare for transition.

there would not be a freshman class. As enrollments began climbing, the Fort Wayne Community Schools converted to a six-three-three program, moving the ninth grade (freshman year) into the junior high, thus creating a three-year high school. The sophomore class in the autumn of 1962 which numbered 423 students was one of the largest classes in the school history. In the fall of 1962 at the South Side-Elmhurst football game, Jane Augspurger was crowned as South Side's first homecoming queen. Her court was made up of Marla Habecker and Tonya Hines.[7] In the early 1960's, there were significant departures and additions to the South Side faculty. In 1961, longtime business teacher Nell Covalt retired and was replaced by Ralph Boling who would spend many years as a teacher and administrator at South Side. In the autumn of 1961, Robert Kelly, who would later become the architect and mentor of South Side's highly successful speech teams, joined the faculty as a business teacher. The year 1962 saw several significant retirements as long-time instructors Russell Furst, Olive Perkins, Pearl Rehorst and Grace Welty, all members of the Quarter Century Club, ended their teaching careers at South Side. Mr. Furst was replaced by Leon Dolby who would become a quarter century faculty member.[8] In the early 1960's, long-time teachers such as Wilburn Wilson, Earl Sterner, Stanley Post, Wayne Scott, Mary Graham, Lucy Osborne, Lester Hostetler, Mabel Fortney, Mary Crowe, Edith Crowe, George Collyer and Clyde Peirce were still members of the faculty. Ora Davis was guidance director, and Pauline VanGorder entered her second decade as dean of girls. Due to the presence of Ora Davis' son, George Robert Davis, on the faculty, Ora Davis was known as "Mr. Davis Upstairs" and George Robert Davis was known as "Mr. Davis Downstairs." In the autumn of 1961, Jack Weicker, a ten-year history teacher, was named "College Counselor" in response to the growing complexity of details that plagued South Side's multitude of college bound students.[9]

Undoubtedly, the most noteworthy event occurring at South Side High School in the early 1960's was the retirement of Principal R. Nelson Snider who had guided South Side High School since 1926. As with most things in his life, Mr. Snider planned his retirement very carefully and gave extreme thought to the question of who should be his successor. One day near the end of the 1961-62 school year, Mr. Snider asked Jack Weicker if he could have lunch with superintendent of schools Lester Grile and himself at the Carriage Inn, a popular restaurant located on South Clinton Street near Oakdale. After receiving this invitation, Jack Weicker recalls that he told his wife, "I'm either going to get fired or I'm going to get a promotion." At the luncheon, Lester Grile indicated that R. Nelson Snider was going to retire at the end of the 1962-63 school year, and that Mr. Snider would like Jack Weicker to succeed him. Mr. Weicker spent the entire 1962-63 school year going through intensive training under the tutelage of Mr. Snider. In January of 1963, Jack Weicker became South Side High School's first assistant principal.[10]

Under the leadership of general manager Susan Smith and advisor James Rohrabaugh, the *South Side Times* published an unprecedented 64-page special edition to honor the retirement of R. Nelson Snider. This Special Edition, dated May 31, 1963, featured a large photograph of Mr. Snider which covered almost the entire front page. The headline read, "Your School Salutes You, Mr. Snider."[11] In recognition of his retirement, tributes to R. Nelson Snider poured in from all over the world. William C. Rastetter, Jr., a graduate of the class of 1927 (the first to graduate under the principalship of Mr. Snider), was named chairman of a farewell banquet scheduled to take place Saturday evening, June 8, 1963, in the Allen County War Memorial Coliseum. The Coliseum was chosen as the only venue in the city of Fort Wayne which could handle the huge crowd anticipated for this event.[12] The Snider retirement dinner was attended by 1,200 persons. People unable to attend the meal were seated in the arena of the Coliseum for the program following the banquet. Sections of seats were designated for certain graduating classes, and a crowd of between 4,000 and 5,000 people participated in the evening program.[13]

On the final day of school in June, 1963, R. Nelson Snider walked out of the doors of South Side High School and into the pages of history. To say that Mr. Snider was a "legend in his time" is to understate the case. His reputation as an educator certainly went beyond the boundaries of the city of Fort Wayne and the state of Indiana. Mildred Luse, long-time South Side High School mathematics teacher,

Mary Graham

recalls an educational conference in the state of Connecticut in the 1950's. She was seated at a table with about a dozen other educators and they were in the process of introducing themselves. When Mrs. Luse introduced herself to the group, and indicated that she was from South Side High School, one of the eastern educators promptly replied, "Isn't that R. Nelson Snider's school?"[14] Ora Davis, former athletic director and long-time guidance director who served under R. Nelson Snider during his entire 37-year principalship, offered these comments concerning Mr. Snider, "He has always insisted that nothing is more important than scholastic endeavors. One of his philosophic tenets to which he has ever clung is that a student must be constantly pressed to achieve his highest scholastic potential. Even failure in a subject has never been allowed to permit a student to drop to a lower level of an academic goal. If a student is capable of high achievement, he must produce high achievement."[15] Paul Sidell, former head of the math department at South Side, stated unequivocally that R. Nelson Snider was the greatest school man he ever knew due primarily to the fact that he was a great organizer.[16]

Mary Graham, a 1929 graduate of South Side High School and a member of the faculty for more than 30 years, also stated "Mr. Snider was a master of organization and always saw the big picture and the bottom line." Miss Graham recalls at the conclusion of the twenty-fifth anniversary program in 1947, all of the seniors were supposed to march out of the main exit doors of the gym, but instead a few people started going out the side doors by the shower rooms and the rest of the senior class in somewhat of a state of disarray followed the leaders out the side doors. Miss Graham said she was absolutely crushed and the first person she ran into was Mr. Snider who had a big smile on his face and said, "Wasn't that program absolutely wonderful?"[17] A man who knew R. Nelson Snider quite well based upon more than a decade of service under him, including close contact during an intense training period to become his successor was, of course, Jack Weicker. Commenting on Mr. Snider, Jack Weicker stated that he was a "no nonsense guy" and "tough as nails but fair." "Kids learned that he was fair but you did not fool around with him. He ran the school with an iron hand and believed that school existed to provide kids with an education." One of Jack Weicker's mentors and advisors was Wilburn Wilson, long-time head of the Social Studies Department and colleague of R. Nelson Snider. Jack Weicker recalls that Mr. Wilson, who had quotes on virtually everything, offered the following comment on R. Nelson Snider, "It was a good thing that people didn't know his first name was Roy because a person with a name like Roy would not go very far." One of Mr. Snider's final comments to Jack Weicker as he turned the reigns of the principalship over to him was, "Thank God I'll never have to attend another *?#! ball game."[18]

The 1963 *Totem* commenting on Mr. Snider's thirty-seven year tenure as principal of South Side High School stated, "Mr. Snider came to South Side with a vision, the dream that he would one day see this educational institution worthy of the great responsibilities entrusted to it and capable of fulfilling its obligation to the youth of America. This vision has been achieved! South Side is renown as one of the nation's finest high schools, and Mr. Snider is recognized as the person behind the product. His strong motives, high standards, unrelenting determination and acute foresight have enabled thousands of young people to enter into the adult world well equipped to meet the challenges of modern times."[19] R. Nelson Snider was to enjoy an active retirement for many years. When he died in March of 1976, he was eulogized by community leaders, and many former students who recalled that he was someone who had really made a difference in their lives. Joining Mr. Snider in retirement in June of 1963 were veteran teachers and Quarter Century Club members Mabel Fortney, Lucy Osborne and Earl Sterner.

B. Jack Weicker Takes Command

As South Side High School opened its doors in September of 1963, an era had ended but an exciting new chapter was to begin. It is difficult to imagine that any person could have greater qualifications or have been better prepared than Jack Weicker to assume the principalship of South Side High School. Mr. Weicker graduated from Harlan High School in 1942 as valedictorian of his class. (He is quick to point out that there were 27 people in his graduating class.) The graduation speech at Harlan High School in 1942 was delivered by R. Nelson Snider. At Indiana University, Mr. Weicker graduated Magna Cum Laude with a degree in history and English. In recognition of his high academic achievement, he was elected to the prestigious Phi Beta Kappa honorary scholastic fraternity. During the 1947-48 school year, he taught history and English at Harrison Hill. In the fall of 1948, he went back to graduate school at IU on what was supposed to be a one-year leave of absence which actually turned out to be a three year leave. During those years of graduate study at Indiana University, he won distinction as a James Albert Woodburn Fellow, an All University Fellow, and a graduate assistant in history. When Jack Weicker returned to Fort Wayne in 1951, he not only had earned his masters degree but had actually completed work on his doctorate. He talked to then superintendent of schools Merle J. Abbett who directed him to South Side High School for a meeting with R. Nelson Snider. Following this discussion with Mr. Snider, he was in turn directed to Wilburn Wilson who was head of the Social Studies Department. Young Jack Weicker and Wilburn Wilson became instant friends and remained such until the death of Mr. Wilson in 1976.[20] Jack Weicker taught history at South Side High School from 1951 to 1961. In 1961, he was named college counselor, and in 1962 was hand picked by R. Nelson Snider as his successor. In January of 1963, he was designated as the first assistant principal in the history of South Side. Mr. Weicker served as principal at South Side High School until his retirement in 1990. The total length of his tenure as principal was 27 years, and the total time spent at South Side was 39 years. A gifted writer, Mr. Weicker has authored numerous publications including a history textbook entitled, *Indiana, The Hoosier State*. Ball State University awarded him the Principal of the Year Award, and the Indiana School Administrators and the Indiana Association of Educational Secretaries bestowed upon him Outstanding Principal of the Year and Indiana Administrator of the Year awards.

During the early years of Jack Weicker's principalship which encompassed the mid 1960's, there were significant developments on the national scene such as the assassination of President John F. Kennedy, growing involvement on the part of the United States in the Vietnam War and the intensification of the civil rights movement. Among the new teachers joining the South Side faculty in the first year of Jack Weicker's principalship in the fall of 1963 was James Tarr, 1951 graduate of South Side who was to teach in the Industrial Arts Department for more than 25 years. Notable retirements in 1964 were Mary Crowe, completing 39 years of service as a history teacher, and Ora Davis completing 40 years of service at South Side. Actually, Ora Davis retired 41 years after joining the faculty during the second year of South Side's existence but he took a leave of absence during the 1945-46 school year to serve as principal of a high school in Arizona.[21] The combined years of experience of Ora Davis and Mary Crowe at South Side totalled 79 years. Joining the South Side faculty in 1964 as publications advisor was Anne White who replaced Keith Wellman, who had served in that position for one year. Mr. Wellman had replaced James Rohrabaugh who was named City Director of Publications.[22] Other new faculty members in the autumn of 1964 were Lois Holtmeyer, a 1940 graduate of South Side, and Don C. Locke, who became South Side's first African American faculty member and taught Social Studies.

In his second year at the helm of South Side High School, during the 1964-65 school year, Jack Weicker began to reorganize and create a sophisticated guidance system in response to the changed needs of students and ever increasing numbers wishing to attend college. In the autumn of 1964, Richard Block was named Dean of Students, while Sam Jackson was named Guidance Coordinator. Pauline VanGorder remained Dean of Girls.[23] Under a new principal in the mid 1960's, South Side traditions were alive and well. Nancy Stewart and Marianne Harper were winners of the Randolph Jacobs Service Trophy during this period.[24] Academic achievement flourished at South Side in the mid 1960's. Among the national merit finalists were Denny Gilbert, Jim Mittelstadt, Tom Robertson, Dennis Bade, George Sherman, Steve Gates, Dick Astrom, Margaret Diehl, Mark Lowens, Mickey Goldstein and Teena Tuenge. With a record of 11 national merit finalists (better than 2% of the class), mean SAT verbal and math scores of 487 and 564 and a college attendance rate of 62% of the senior class, South Side was academically unique.[25]

Richard Block

Among the clubs at South Side in the mid 1960's were the Archery Club, Art Club, Assemblies Workshop, Band, Booster, Bridge, Choir, Cinema Guild (a new club in 1964-65), Hi-Y, Junior Academy of Science, Latin Club, Letterman's Club, Library Club, Majorettes, Meterites, National Honor Society, Pegasus, Philo, Political Science, Quill and Scroll, Red Cross, Rifle, Safety Council, *Times*, *Totem*, Usher Club, Vesta, Visual Education, Wranglers, Yell Club and Y Teens.[26]

During the mid 1960's, the tradition of a strong music program continued at South Side. Lester Hostetler continued to do a stellar job as director of vocal music, and Robert Drummond was in his second decade as director of instrumental music. In athletics, South Side teams continued rebuilding programs. The 1964 football team won only two games, although the reserve team lost only one game which should have been a tipoff as to what was to come in the near future. During the 1964-65 basketball season, the team did not post a winning record, but senior guard Denny Peppler received All City honors. Another member of that team named to the All City squad was a young sophomore named Willie Long.[27]

1961 – Hi-Y's Queen of Hearts Dance

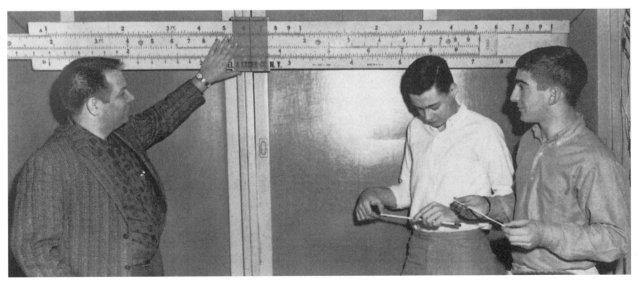

Richard Bussard explains the slide rule.

The freedom shrine for South Side's World War II veterans establishes a basis for pride and security in Kelly students Ann LaMar, Gonzalo Godoy and Jane Campbell.

In 1965, Frank Geist replaced Robert Gernand as track coach, Everett Havens was still tennis coach and Robert Drummond returned as golf coach after having turned the reigns over for a few years to Warren Hoover. Veteran teachers in the physical education department were Alice Keegan, who was still directing the Girls Athletic Association, and Clair Motz, who guided the splendid intramural program.[28] The class of 1965 graduated more than 550 students and had the distinction of being the largest graduating class up to that time in South Side history. Sally Henderson had served three consecutive years as president of the class of 1965.[29]

C. Dress Codes and Vietnam

In the mid 1960's, national attention focused on President Johnson's escalation of American involvement in Vietnam. There were student protests in every section of the country. The Supreme Court of the United States rendered various decisions concerning the type of clothing students should wear to class. At South Side High School, the Snider era had past into the euphoria of yesterday, and the Weicker era promised optimism and achievement. On the athletic field, South Side High School was poised to enter another golden age, perhaps brighter than those of the late 30's and early 40's and even brighter than those of the mid to late 50's. These previous golden ages of athletics were largely confined to one sport, basketball, and were not necessarily shared by the football and track teams. In the golden age of the mid to late 60's, South Side was to produce a state finalist basketball team, an undefeated football team, and a boys state track championship. Significant faculty retirements in June of 1965 included Edith Crowe, Ruth Fleck, Paul Sidell and Wilburn Wilson. Mr. Wilson, chairman of the Social Studies Department, had 39 years of service at South Side, Mr. Sidell, head of the Math Department, had 37 years of service, and Edith Crowe, a health teacher, had 35 years of service at the time of her retirement. At the Junior Banquet held in December of 1965, junior class president, Jim Lohman, introduced former Principal R. Nelson Snider who was the speaker. In addition, there was a skit entitled, "Secret Agent," and the participants were Carolyn Russ, Barb Kelly, Liffy Keck, Sandy Moyer, Sandee Foelber, Steve Powell and a young Archer actress who was to achieve fame in television and motion pictures by the name of Shelley Long. Retiring in June of 1966 were two additional faculty members who had come to South Side in the late 1930's. These retirees were Alice Keegan, who started teaching at South Side in 1937 and Clyde Peirce, who began his South Side teaching career in 1938.[30]

New additions to the faculty in the fall of 1966 included Daniel Boylan and Ned Yingst, both of whom would teach more than 25 years at South Side. William Hedges joined the faculty as a Social Studies teacher. He later became head of the Social Studies Department, as well as assistant principal and remained at South Side for 25 years.[31] Another new faculty member joining the staff in 1966 was Neal Thomas, a 1953 graduate of South Side High School. Mr. Thomas also would remain on the faculty more than 25 years. During the 1966-67 school year, Principal Jack Weicker continued to streamline the administrative staff as well as the curriculum. Richard Block was appointed assistant principal, and Ralph Boling became dean of boys. Pauline VanGorder was serving her last year as dean of girls and would retire in June of 1967. Miss VanGorder had served in that position since 1950 when she replaced the original dean of girls, Martha Pittenger. Pauline VanGorder who will be remembered for many noteworthy contributions to South Side, including her chairmanship of the highly successful savings bond drives during World War II had originally come to South Side in January of 1929. She concluded 38 1/2 years of service.[32] Miss VanGorder was to enjoy a highly productive retirement for nearly 30 years during which time she remained an ardent booster of South Side High School and all of its activities. She passed away at the age of 95 in April of 1996. Many new special classes were established during the 1966-67 academic year. These classes consisted of sophomores, juniors and seniors chosen by their teachers who participated in

Shelley Long

accelerated courses in chemistry, government, English and mathematics. In some of these classes, teaching techniques were changed and the method of "team teaching" was employed for the first time at South Side. During this year, classes rotated from teacher to teacher. In this manner, instructors taught only their preferred subjects and many times only their specialty in a certain subject area. One of the greatest accomplishments of the 1966-67 academic year was the high rating received by South Side from the North Central Association. The evaluation committee report stated that South Side was a good strong school.[33]

In the spring of 1967, senior Shelley Long was serving as president of Wranglers and was the winner of the Rotary Speech Contest. Her coach was South Side speech instructor Robert Storey.[34] South Side traditions were alive and well in the mid 1960's. The Service Club was still awarding the Randolph Jacobs Trophy donated by the family in memory of a South Side student who lost his life in World War II. In 1965, this award was won by Marianne Simmons and Nancy Cooper.[35] This award was won in 1966 by Debbie Shaw.[36] The 1966 Homecoming Queen was Jan Jones, while in 1967 the tradition of the Hi-Y Queen of Hearts selection continued with Sally Reidtorf being crowned as queen and Jim Wallis being chosen as King Kelly.[37] One of South Side's most revered traditions, Ivy Day, entered its fourth decade as Cindy Osborne became the thirtieth Ivy Day Queen in 1965.[38] She was succeeded by Toya O'Hora in 1966 and Jan Jones in 1967. The 1967 Ivy Day court consisted of Shelley Long, Sally Reidtorf, Liffy Keck and Linda Young.[39] At the conclusion of the 1966-67 school year, the Music Department continued to present outstanding programs, both in the areas of instrumental and vocal music which were headed by Robert Drummond and Lester Hostetler respectively. By 1967, Mr. Drummond and Mr. Hostetler had compiled nearly fifty years of combined experience at South Side High School.[40]

The 1964 Archer football team won only two games including the last game of the season when they defeated Central Catholic 7-6. The 1964 reserve team was extremely promising losing only one game. In 1965 when these reserve players became members of the varsity, the South Side football team posted the second undefeated season in school history by winning all nine of their scheduled games, including an exciting one point victory over Central Catholic in the season finale. This 1965 undefeated football team which won nine games eclipsed the record eight game victory seasons held by the 1932, 1933 and 1944 Archer football squads. Two juniors were standouts on the 1965 undefeated football team. Barry Worman won the city scoring title, and fullback Tom Fleming finished second in city scoring. Worman and Fleming were selected to All State as well as All City teams along with Ned Melchi and Eric Danley who were also selected to the First Team All City squad.[41] Other standout players on this 1965 undefeated Archer football team were Steve Hower, Kerry Kaplan, John Leakey, Ron Christon, Art Walker, Jim Lohman, Dan Nolan, and Mike Fraizer.[42] The 1965 football team was ranked fifth in the state at the end of the season. In 1966, many of the stars from the previous year returned. The 1966 squad won their first eight games thus running their consecutive winning streak to eighteen over a period of three seasons, a South Side High School record.[43] The 1966 football team lost a heartbreaker in the final game of the season to Central Catholic by a score of 24-20 to finish the season with eight victories and one defeat. The team at one time was ranked as high as third in the state and finished the season ranked seventh in the state. The standouts of the 1966 football squad were Barry Worman, Tom Fleming, John Mumy, and Mike Danley, all of whom were elected First Team All City as well as Dan Nolan, John Dunfee, Scott Lougheed, Jesse Booker, Dave Junk, Chip Smith, Steve Hower, Jim Ule, Jim Lohman and Greg Gaulden.[44] The 1967 football team posted a sparkling seven win, two loss record. In three football seasons (1965, 1966 and 1967), under the masterful coaching of Robert Gernand, South Side won an amazing 24 games while losing only three. The standout player on the 1967 football team was senior fullback Scott Lougheed who won the city scoring title. Scott also placed himself high on the list of South Side's outstanding punters by kicking 29 times for an average of 36 yards and a total of 1,032 yards.[45] Scott Lougheed was later an outstanding player at Purdue University. Other notable players on the 1967 Archer football team were John Lumpp, Bill Watson and Bobby Lucas.

The 1965-66 sports season saw the introduction of wrestling as a varsity sport. The team was coached by Mr. Ray Hyde. Included among the outstanding wrestlers on this first South Side team was Joel Grandstaff who took fourth in the state tournament in his weight division, Jim Brookhart and Tom Brooks won sectional titles in their respective weight division.[46] In 1965, Don Reichert began his 15th season as Archer basketball coach making him the longest tenured net coach in school history. The 1965-66 team featured perhaps the greatest Archer basketball player in history in the person of junior Willie Long. This team had just a so-so season record winning 13 and losing seven but they caught fire in the tournament. They won the sectional title (South Side's first since 1961)

Willie Long

1965 Undefeated football team.

1967 Semi-State Basketball Champs

1965 Undefeated football team.

and the regional championship (South Side's first since 1959). In the semi-state, they lost by one point to Anderson. Other outstanding players on the 1965-66 basketball team were John Leakey, Steve Bryant, Dan Nolan, Jim Wallis andChuck Nelson.[47]

The 1966-67 basketball campaign with many veteran players returning promised to be a good season. These promises were fulfilled as this team compiled a great season. Led by Willie Long who was "Mr. Everything," the Archers lost only three regular season games. In the first game of the sectional tournament, they won a thrilling 66-65 overtime victory from Central. In this game, Willie Long, Jim Wallis, and Dan Nolan all left the game due to fouls. In the overtime period, Chuck Nelson was the star who ensured victory.[48] The Archers then won their second consecutive regional crown, and the following week defeated defending state champion Michigan City and always dangerous Marion to advance to the state finals for the sixth time in school history.[49] In the afternoon game of the state finals, Willie Long got into foul trouble as a result of some questionable calls by the officials. He fouled out with three minutes and 52 seconds to go in the third quarter and South Side lost to Lafayette Jeff 79-70.[50] After the final game of the state tournament, it was announced that Chuck Nelson of South Side had been awarded the coveted Arthur L. Trester Award for mental attitude and outstanding ability. Chuck Nelson became the first and only Archer to win this award.[51] Willie Long, arguably the greatest individual player to ever wear an Archer basketball uniform, concluded his career with 1,697 points, a career South Side record, and he was name to the All State team and also received the honor of "Mr. Basketball." He wore jersey #1 in the Indiana-Kentucky All Star Game. Following his graduation from South Side, Long had a successful college career and played in the National Basketball Association with the Denver Nuggets.

The 1967 track team had one of the best seasons in recent years. The team finished eighth at the

1967 state track and field meet as John Lumpp finished second in the 440 yard dash and Tom Fleming finished second in the shot put.[52] The following track season was perhaps the most surprising in South Side history as the Archers won the 1968 state track and field championship in one of the greatest upsets of all time. The coaches of this team were Pres Brown, Tom Lindenburg and Walt Bartkiewicz. After winning the sectional, the Archers finished only fourth in the regional tournament and qualified only a few individuals for the state finals. Due to the small number of individuals who qualified for the state track and field finals, South Side could only have scored a possible 26 points. This small band of Archers proceeded to score 20 points which was enough to win the 1968 state track championship. John Lumpp won first place in the 440 with the outstanding time of 48.2, up to that time, the best ever run by a Fort Wayne athlete. The mile relay team composed of Randy Rhoades, Paul Dekker, Bill Watson and John Lumpp finished second. Scott Lougheed placed second in the pole vault and Bill Watson finished fourth in the 440.[53]

The Autumn of 1967 saw significant changes in the administration of South Side High School. Jack Weicker was beginning his fifth year as principal with Richard Block as assistant principal. Ralph Boling was in his second year as Dean of Boys and Mary Smith was the new Dean of Girls replacing Pauline VanGorder. Mary Graham, a twenty-five year veteran of the English Department, assumed the duties of college counselor. Thomas Gordon became guidance coordinator. The Girls Athletic Association also had a new leader, Jeanette Rohleder, who replaced Alice Keegan. Don Reichert relinquished the post of head basketball coach after sixteen extremely successful seasons which saw his Archer teams win seven sectional titles, six regional crowns, two semi-state championships and one state title.[54] Don Reichert coached more basketball victories than any other mentor in South Side history. Mr. Reichert was succeeded as head basketball coach in 1967 by Charles "Porky" Holt.[55] Amid numerous faculty and administrative changes, Robert Drummond and Lester Hostetler guided instrumental and vocal music in the autumn of 1967. Clarence Murray, long-time industrial arts teacher, moved to the guidance staff in the area of vocational guidance, and Clair Motz completed 15 years as head of the intramural pro-

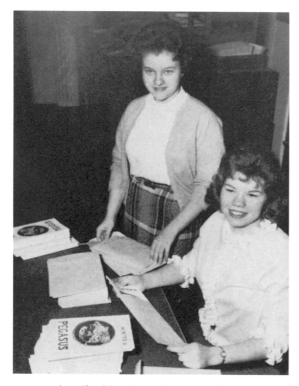

Jennifer Manth and Kaylene Gilbert

Chuck Nelson along with his mother receives
A.L. Trester Award.

gram. Teachers who had come to South Side during the late 1930's and were still on the faculty included Stanley Post, Ernest Walker and George Collyer. Wayne Scott, former head basketball coach, had completed 25 years at South Side and was still serving as athletic director.[56] The 1967 tennis team coached by Everett Havens won the city championship and had an outstanding record of 11 wins and two losses.[57] In the late 1960's, a language laboratory was functioning at South Side. Through the use of earphones, teachers were able to emphasize the audio lingual phase of foreign language. The students in turn were able to test their comprehension by listening to recordings.[58] Those things which were unchanging served as mainstays for Archer students. Such was the case with South Side tradition. Customs and activities which could be traced far back through the history of South Side were still part of the school. The Randolph Jacobs service cup was still being presented at the annual service club potluck, crowns were still bestowed upon the Homecoming Queen, Ivy Day Queen, Hi-Y Queen of Hearts and King Kelly. The annual Hi-Y bonfire followed the South Side-Central Catholic game bringing the football season to a close.[59] On the club scene at South Side in the late 1960's, some of the old standbys such as Philo, Meterites, Wranglers, Letterman's and Hi-Y still continued. In addition, other clubs appeared such as the Bridge Club, Cinema Club, and a brand new club, the Afro American Club which was to become one of South Side's strongest and most dominant organizations. At the end of the 1960's, South Side rejuvenated the idea of the Student Council after Principal Jack Weicker formulated a constitution.[60] Academic achievement continued at South Side as Christopher Walker, Carol Lake, Diane Farhi, Lee Johnson, Greg Wass, Marta Graff and Nancy Howard all qualified for final competition in the National Merit Scholarship Program.[61]

In the fall of 1968, Norman Hobson became South Side's first African American class president as he was chosen to lead the senior class of 1969. Among the graduates of this class were Nancy Eshcoff (now Boyer) who became the first female judge of the Allen Superior Court and Martin Erickson who would later join the South Side faculty. Also in the fall of 1968, Bill Walker became South Side's new cross country and track coach. Another new faculty member in the autumn of 1968 was Richard Melton who would remain for many years on the South Side faculty as a math teacher, tennis coach and golf coach.[62] The 1968 football team had another successful season winning six and losing three. Coached by Robert Gernand, they used the single wing and were led by senior fullback Bill Watson. First Team All City selections were Bill Watson and guardRandy Wamsley and Second Team All City Selections were Tom Snider and John Fisher. The Archer basketball teams under Charles "Porky" Holt were rebuilding and managed few victories. One of the standout players on South Side's basketball teams of the late 60's was Tim Reitdorf who averaged 17.6 games per year in the 1968-69 basketball season and earned a birth on the All City team.[63] The 1969 junior Totem editors were Cindy Hess, Jeanne Keck, Shirley McEachern and Nancy Snyderman who was later to become famous as Dr. Nancy Snyderman, nationally prominent author and frequent host on ABC television's

1968 State Track Champions. First row: Teague and Stuerzenberger. Second row: Dekker, Borgmann, Lougheed, Watson, Lumpp, Rhoades, Duff and Wamsley.

"Good Morning America."[64] In June of 1969, Lester Hostetler retired after 29 years as director of vocal music. Later that summer, the United States placed a man on the moon, and in the autumn of 1969, Juanita Mendenhall joined the faculty as a home economics teacher.[65] Mrs. Mendenhall was to teach at South Side for 25 years and would institute extremely innovative programs designed to assist students in financial management, family life, and other aspects of navigating in the real world. As the decade of the 1960's ended, South Side High School was ready to enter its sixth decade of service to the community.

John Theye and Nancy Snyderman

Enlivened lunch hours result when Seniors Susie Holland, Candy Sommers, and Dottie Gallmeister slip in a little time for television.

The planting of the United States flag on the moon on July 20, 1969, symbolized a milestone in mankind's history. Astronaut Edwin E. Aldrin, Jr., lunar module pilot, poses for a photograph, taken by Astronaut Neil A. Armstrong, commander (NASA).

CHAPTER SIX
1970 - 1979

A. Finally, An Auditorium

The 1970 *Totem* aptly described life at South Side High School as the new decade opened: "We studied together, pelted each other with snow balls and cheered at a basketball game until we were hoarse. Arguing about the Vietnam War, racial tensions or politics, we formed a set a values and convictions that we would carry outside the walls of South Side. We found a happiness that comes with sharing whether it was advice, a problem or a funny experience. Together we concocted strange potions in chemistry, slid down ramps and fashioned posters for club meetings. We experienced the delight of a good report card, the anticipation of a stimulating class, and sighs of relief after a midterm test. Using the knowledge, guidance and friendship offered at South Side, we developed as individuals as well as a student body."[1]

The decade of the 70's was to see the usual array of significant national events. American involvement in Vietnam would end as would the draft. For the first time in our nation's history, a president would resign and would be succeeded by a chief executive who had never been elected vice president. At South Side High School, old traditions continued, new ones were conceived and some of the old fixtures such as the football stadium disappeared. Early in 1970, senior Willie Simmons accepted the Valentine King scepter and Jan Hines was voted Queen of Hearts. Jeanette Suttle received the crown of Afro-American Queen.[2] The Archer basketball team under Coach Charles "Porky" Holt won ten and lost ten and was eliminated in its first tournament game. In the spring of 1970, the track team under Coach Bill Walker had one of their finest seasons finishing third at the state track meet.[3] On the golf links, Robert Drummond was still the golf coach in the spring of 1970 as he had been since the late 1940's (except for a brief period in the late 60's when Warren Hoover was golf coach). The year of 1970 was billed as a rebuilding year for the golf team due to the graduation in 1969 of All City Team members Tom Motter, Merrill Phillips, Phil Erli and letterman, Ken Cornacchione. The 1969 golf team had won the city championship. Forming the nucleus of the 1970 team were returning veterans Jim Motter and All City Team member Tom Kelley, one of the finest golfers in South Side history.[4] Another excellent Archer golfer Tom Inskeep would shoot a round of 72 a year later at Cedar Creek Course. His score of 72 was only one

Robert Weber watches as botany students Juniors Ann Spear and Julie Inskeep study the formation of a plant.

stroke off of the school record which had been set by Ken Rodewald in the early 1950's.[5]

In club activities, Robert Weber and the Hi-Y Club continued their long tradition of activities including sponsorship of annual events such as the Best Girl Banquet and the King and Queen of Hearts Dance. The Letterman's Club sponsored by George Robert Davis continued its tradition of helping the Fort Wayne Christmas Bureau by collecting canned goods to be distributed to the homes of the needy during the Christmas season.[6] The Junior Classical League which was in its third year gave Latin students an opportunity to enjoy themselves while learning about ancient Greek and Roman civilization. JCL sponsored the annual Roman Banquet and was headed by Lois Holtmeyer, a 1940 graduate of South Side High School.[7] The long tradition of excellence in publications was continued with both the *Times* and the *Totem*. The editor-in-chief of the 1970 *Totem* was Nancy Snyderman. The senior class of 1970 was mindful of long-time traditions but felt that these traditions should be re-evaluated, and the ones deemed worthy kept and those outdated replaced. Among those traditions changed in 1970 were the customary gray graduation caps and gowns which were replaced by emerald green and the senior banquet which was exchanged for the senior party that created an informal kind of fun for the class.[8]

In the autumn of 1970, John Meadows, who replaced long-time vocal music director Lester Hostetler, was in his second year. At this time, Mr. Meadows totally revamped the Vocal Music Department. For the first time in the history of the department, there were three performing groups which included the Chorale, the Mixed Chorus and the Girls' Chorus.[9] Among the new faculty members arriving in September of 1970 were Gary Black and Beverly Wheeler[10] (later Beverly Jones). Both of these teachers would remain at South Side High School for 25 years.

On the football field, the 1970 season proved to be nostalgic. Coach Robert Gernand completed his 15th season with a three win five loss record. This football season was extremely significant. It marked the last football game with Central since that school was closing. The Archers lost this final game

1969 – First Afro-American Club

with the Central Tigers by a score of 23-0. A few weeks later in the last game to be played in the old South Side stadium, the Archers scored a 40-15 victory over Central Catholic.[11] South Side stadium, the site of Archer home games since 1923, was scheduled to be drastically revamped and would no longer be used as a football facility. Wayne High School would open in the autumn of 1971, and the Archer home games would be played at Wayne Stadium for nearly 25 years until the opening of Archer Field in 1995. (Principal Jennifer Manth did succeed in scheduling one home game a year in the old stadium facility in the mid 1990's shortly before the opening of Archer Field). In the spring of 1971, baseball appeared as a varsity sport after an absence of 41 years. In June of 1971, South Side lost its final link with the 1930's as Ernest Walker, Stanley Post, and George Collyer retired from the faculty. Mr. Walker and Mr. Post had started their teaching careers at South Side in 1937 while Mr. Collyer came in 1938.[12]

Hall's Drive-In, a favorite meeting place.

When Archer students returned from summer vacation in the autumn of 1971, for the first time in history they could boast that they had their own auditorium. In 1970, a massive construction and renovation program was started at South Side. This program, the most extensive since the addition of the second floor in 1938, was to continue for three years. The members of the class of 1973 spent their entire high school careers at South Side enduring this renovation project. By the autumn of 1971, phase one of the project had been completed. Included in phase one were extensive renovations and additions to the music department, the opening of a completely new library on the second floor above the north entrance where the cafeteria was previously located, and finally in October of 1971 the opening of the splendid auditorium which seated 900 people.[13] The 1971-72 school year was a year of great change at South Side. In addition to the ongoing renovation project, Wayne High School had opened, and several of the South Side teachers transferred to that school. Included among those teachers transferring were Don Reichert, long-time teacher and former basketball coach who became athletic director at Wayne High School and Everett Havens, long-time tennis coach.[14] The 1971-72 school year also marked the rejuvenation of South Side's speech and dramatics department under the capable leadership of Robert Kelly. The auditorium, which opened in October of 1971, was the catalyst of this rejuvenation. The senior class play in the fall of 1971 entitled, "You Can't Take It With You" was presented under the direction of Robert Kelly. During this period, contemporaneous with the renovation and remodeling of classrooms and under the capable direction of Jack Weicker, South Side was beginning to streamline its curriculum. One of the advantages of the renovation was that it allowed centralized location of classrooms according to subject matter area. One of the many innovations introduced by Mr. Weicker during this period was the elimination of the longstanding open lunch periods where students could leave the building for one to two hours. During the 1971-72 school year, the doors were closed and the students were restricted to the building and lunch hours were cut to utilize more time for study.[15] At the Quarter Century Club Banquet in the autumn of 1971, the Meterite girls sang such songs as "Mrs. Robinson" and "Love Story." In honor of the late Rowena Harvey, they sang, "Only A Rose."[16]

There were many new clubs and organizations during the 1971-72 school year. Due to the construction of the new auditorium, a new organization the Masque and Gavel was started by Mr. Robert Kelly. The masque symbolized the theater aspect of the organization and the gavel symbolized speech. Other new clubs appearing during this school year were the Medical Opportunities Club under the direction of Mrs. Juanita Mendenhall and the United Peoples Movement, cosponsored by Mr. John Arnold and Mr. Daniel Boylan. This club was made up of students who wished to break down prejudice in school, home and community.[17]

In January of 1972, phase two of the construction and renovation project began. Featured in this phase were the tearing down of the stadium walls, the installation of an all-weather track, the removal of Darrow Street between Clinton Court and Calhoun and the tearing out of the old study hall and boys and girls locker rooms to make room for the new administrative central offices which would open in the fall of 1972. In addition, a new public address system was installed. The renovation of the main gymnasium also started in 1972 and was completed when the 1972-73 basketball season opened. This gymnasium renovation featured a new floor, reconditioned seats and a new drop ceiling that eliminated the airplane hanger-type rafters that had been in the gym since 1922. In the spring of 1972, head basketball coach Charles "Porky" Holt resigned after serving five years. Archer track teams under the capable guidance of Bill Walker were entering a very productive and successful era. The 1971 track team had experienced an undefeated season and finished fifth at the state track meet.[18] In the Tech Invitational, the Archers defeated seven teams, including state champion Gary Roosevelt. They continued their victories at the North Side Relays trouncing 15 other squads. After capturing top sectional honors, the Archers suffered their first defeat of the season placing second to Elkhart in the regionals. At the state finals in Indianapolis, South Side tied for fifth place. John Brooks captured second place in the mile run. In the

Juanita Mendenhall

Robert Kelly

high jump, Charlie Stewart cleared the bar at 6'-7" to tie but was awarded second place on the basis of fewer misses. Derrick Fowlkes finished fifth in the long jump. Overall, South Side tied for fifth at the 1971 state finals. The following year, 1972, the Archers finished second at the state track meet.[19] Bill Walker would become the most successful boys track coach in South Side history guiding his Archer squads to 114 victories over a 14-year span and finishing second at the state track meet four times (1972, 1978, 1980 and 1981).[20]

B. The Golden Anniversary

The outstanding event of the early 1970's was the celebration of South Side's 50th anniversary. In order to conduct an appropriate celebration of the golden anniversary, principal Jack Weicker started extensive planning one year in advance. Mr. Weicker named Mary Graham, longtime English teacher and guidance counselor, as general chairman of the 50th anniversary steering committee. One year of meticulous planning culminated in the 50th anniversary program which was held on Saturday evening, April 29, 1972, in the new South Side High School auditorium. The coordinator of the anniversary observation was William Hedges, while the director of the auditorium program was Robert Kelly. Evlyn Spray was coordinator of the auditorium program, George Robert Davis was chairman of tours and exhibits, Lois Holtmeyer served as registration chairman and Juanita Mendenhall was reception chairman.[21] Many individuals prominent in the history of South Side participated in the 50th anniversary program. Former principal R. Nelson Snider gave his reminiscences of the early years. Paul Hahn, a graduate of South Side's first class in 1923 and a professor of German at Ohio Wesleyan University, led in the singing of the school

George Robert Davis

song which he had composed during his senior year. The surviving members of the 1938 state championship basketball team, along with their coach Burl Friddle, were honored. Five of the "sweet 16" teachers who began when the school opened in 1922 and remained 25 years or more were present at the ceremony. Pauline VanGorder recalled South Side's participation during the World War II years. John Hoffman, a graduate of the class of 1933, gave a presentation entitled, "A Student Looks Back" while Steve Shine, Dana Bredemeyer and Kate Black presented "Today's Graduates Look Ahead."[22]

In his introductory remarks at the 50th anniversary celebration, Jack Weicker quoted his friend and mentor Wilburn Wilson who said, "I am fast approaching the age when I can remember quite vividly things that had never really happened at all." In addition, Mr. Weicker recalled the comments made by R. Nelson Snider during his last day on the job as he was leaving the South Side building after 37 years as principal. At that time, Mr. Snider said to Mr. Weicker, "Don't be afraid of change in the years ahead. This school has been in the process of change since 1922, and it will continue to change dramatically in the years that stretch out ahead of you." Mr. Weicker commented that in the years immediately before the 50th anniversary, South Side High School had more national merit semi-finalists than all of the other public schools in the city of Fort Wayne and had more Hoosier Scholars in the past five years than all of the other high schools in Allen County combined. At the 1972 anniversary program, Mr. Weicker also talked about student protests. He stated, "I think we at South Side cannot help but be in sympathy with most of the hopes of young people so long as they are using constitutional means to draw attention to their thoughts and ideas. We may not of course always be in accord with the product of their reasoning but we certainly cannot be opposed to the process which supports the idea of essential democracy."[23]

As the students returned to school in September of 1972, the renovation project was nearing completion. The administrative offices had now been moved to the location of the former study hall and boys and girls locker rooms immediately inside the Calhoun Street door. The old botany solarium, a prominent landmark along Oakdale, was eliminated and Robert Weber, the botany teacher, received a brand new classroom and laboratory. The *South Side Times* moved into the location formerly occupied by the Botany Room.[24] (The botany solarium would reappear in its former location in 1996 as part of the most recent renovation project). In November of 1972, many Archers cast their ballots as 18-year olds voting for the first time for President. This election resulted in a second term for Richard Nixon.[25] In the

Pres Brown

autumn of 1972 responding to various federal government directives, the Indiana State Athletic Association decided that for the first time girls could compete in varsity sports. The result was the immediate appearance of variety of girls varsity sports teams at South Side. The first girls team to compete at the varsity level was the volleyball team which was coached in 1972 by Jeanette Rohleder. The team posted a record of six wins and three losses and won two games in the sectional before losing to Heritage.[26]

The 1972 football team under coach Robert Gernand experienced an unusual season winning only one game. The co-captains were Jack Morris and Art Chambers.[27] The 1972 tennis team coached by Richard Melton lost only one match during the regular season and finished as runners-up in the sectional. Rick Hanauer and Bruce Curley were a very effective doubles combination for the Archers.[28] In 1972, Murray Mendenhall, a member of Central's 1943 state championship basketball team became South Side's boys basketball coach. His first team had a winning season but was defeated in the first game of the sectional by North Side.[29] Glen Stebing, former varsity basketball coach and long-time faculty member, took over the intramural program in 1972 as Clair Motz retired after 20 very successful years. A new addition to the faculty during the 1972-73 school year was Frances Gooden, an English teacher.[30] Mrs. Gooden would remain at South Side for more than 20 years, eventually becoming assistant principal. In June of 1973, Wayne Scott retired after 31 years at South Side.[31] Mr. Scott held the athletic director's position for 22 years and was succeeded by Pres Brown who had been a member of the South Side faculty for several years. Mr. Brown would hold the athletic director's position for an additional 21 years.[32] Following the retirement of Wayne Scott, Mary Graham became the longest tenured faculty member. She joined the faculty in 1942 and had completed 33 years on the staff at the time of Wayne Scott's retirement. In the autumn of 1973, the boys cross country team under the direction of Bill Walker compiled an impressive record of 24 wins and 3 losses, which was the second best record in school history. At the state meet, the cross country team finished third. Members of this outstanding team included John Cottrell, Kim Rudolf, Ken Hogan and Matt Wyneken. Girls varsity sports during the 1973-74 school year now consisted of volleyball, gymnastics, and tennis. The South Side girls tennis team finished first in the city in the 1973 season. Members of this championship team were Melaine Thexton, Ann Johnson, Dane Bromelmeier, Susan Houser, Sue Becker, Leslie Koehlinger, Sally McNagny, Jan Fields and Pam Fisher.[33] The girls varsity gymnastics team in its first year of competition in 1973 won the sectional tournament, and Cheryl Barnes was the state vaulting champion.[34] Murray Mendenhall's boys varsity basketball team in 1973-74 won South Side's first sectional in seven years. Jeff Hallgren, Reggie Burt and Cornelius Hill were named to the All City team. Additional members of 1973-74 boys varsity basketball team were Craig Taylor and Gregg Taylor, who would later return to South Side as basketball coaches.[35] In the autumn of 1973, South Side High School inducted the first members into its Athletic Hall of Fame. Included among the first inductees was former principal R. Nelson Snider.[36]

As the renovation and construction project was completed, and as the curriculum was streamlined, new clubs and activities developed at South Side. A math lab was established in the center of the Math Department which offered calculators for students to use. In addition to calculators, the math lab also contained film strips that explained problem areas of every math subject.[37] By 1974, the Business Department had been greatly supplemented by the cooperative office education program which allowed students majoring in secretarial practice to get "on the job" training. The students went to South Side in the morning for classes, and in the afternoon they went to work in an office. Home Economic students learned to improve their lives. Human Development students learned about their personal adjustment through the study and observation of the development of man through life. A day care center for small children was open and through this, classes were able to observe directly. One of the leaders in the Human Development program was Mrs. Juanita Mendenhall, a Home Economics teacher.[38] Among the new clubs instituted during the 1973-74 school year was the Word Club which was formed to help students build their vocabulary through the study of suffixes, prefixes and roots. Lois Holtmeyer was the sponsor of this club.[39] In addition, Spirit Week, which had been instituted in 1972, had its second celebration beginning on Monday, November 19, 1973. In the spring of 1974, Matt Wyneken set a school record for the two-mile run with a time of 9:27.2.[40] The 1974 baseball team coached by Don Waldrop made more hits, scored more runs, and had a better fielding average then any other team since South Side resumed baseball as an interscholastic sport in 1971. The 1974 baseball team finished as runners-up in the SAC. Dick Boggess and Chuck Brown were named to the All SAC First Team.[41]

Richard M. Nixon

C. Presidents Don't Resign, Do They?

When South Side students returned to school in September of 1974, the nation had a new president. The previous August, Richard Nixon became the first president in United States history to resign. He was replaced by Gerald R. Ford who became Vice President after Spiro Agnew's resignation in 1973. Gerald Ford became the first president in our history who had not been elected as Vice President. A shortage of gasoline continued to plagued the nation in the autumn of 1974 pushing prices for the first time over 50 cents per gallon.[42] The fashions of the mid 1970's were in evidence at South Side High School. Skirts fell below the knee and buttoned up the front. Long dresses at floor length were popular for weddings, dances and parties. Pants that were very dressy pajamas became suitable to entertain party guests. High wasted baggies with cuffed bottoms made the scene for both men and women. These pants sometimes decorated with sequins and embroidery were made of corduroy, velvet and of course good ole blue jean denim. Shoes were the hottest items on the market. Clogs were big with very high heels. Earth shoes with the thicker sole at the toe were coming into style. Perhaps the strangest looking shoe was the "moon shoe." This was a clog-type shoe where the upper part was about 1/2 inch thick.[43] Rock music was still the most popular type among teenagers. Elvis Presley, the super star of the 50's was still around although less important. The Beatles were making a go of it as individuals with Paul McCartney having the most success. Only the "Rolling Stones" and the "Hollies" remained of the British rock groups that took the country by storm in the mid 1960's. John Denver led the country western singers while Gladys Knight and the Pips, James Brown and Aretha Franklin shared the soul spot light. The new musical groups were led by "Bachman-Turner Overdrive."[44]

In the autumn of 1974, there was not only a change in the national administration in Washington D.C., but principal Jack Weicker beginning his twelfth year as chief administrator at South Side High School continued making innovative changes. By the 1974-75 school year, the positions of Dean of Men and Dean of Women were eliminated and the administration was headed by Mr. Weicker as principal, and Richard Block as assistant principal. Ralph Boling and Dorothy Walters were assistants to the principal. Thomas Gordon continued as guidance coordinator with Pres Brown, Mary Graham, and former South Side athletic star Dan Nolan as counselors. In the mid 1970's, thanks in large part to the addition of the auditorium, the South Side Speech and Drama Department continued to flourish under the excellent leadership of Robert Kelly. In the autumn of 1974, the senior class play entitled, "Flowers For Algernon" was performed on two different nights attracting nearly 1,000 people and raising $1,400 for the senior class. The male lead was played by Brian Teixeira and Rosemarie Picht was cast in the female lead. Throughout the mid 1970's, South Side had a very successful speech team. Mr. Kelly and the team members braved bad weather, long bus rides and arising at 5:30 a.m., to attend many Saturday meets. They participated in such diverse categories as humorous interpretation, poetry, original oratory, oratorical declamation, dramatic interpretation and dramatic duo. Included among the outstanding members of the speech team in the mid 1970's were Terry McCaffrey, Martha Lampe and Christy Miller.[45] In 1975, the senior class play, again directed by Mr. Robert Kelly, was a success when James Reach's drama entitled, "David and Lisa" was performed with Lynn Wehrenberg and Steven Holley appearing in the title roles.[46]

Spirit Week, which had been originated in 1972, continued to be a highlight on the student calendar at South Side during the mid 1970's. On "Dress Down Day" the school looked like a line at the Unemployment Bureau. "Wild Hats and Socks Day" turned up big brims and sombreros as well as stripes and plaids. On "Lick Em Day" students spent the whole day with suckers or jaw breakers. Other activities included a picture guessing contest with baby pictures of the football team which was won by Brian Link and a sexy legs contest held among the seniors on the basketball team which was won by Craig Taylor. Craig was awarded a pair of pantyhose for his efforts.[47] For the first time in South Side's history, the senior class of 1975 held their banquet in a Chinese restaurant. Chop sticks proved to be an interesting chal-

1973 Marching Band

lenge as principal Jack Weicker and assistant principal Richard Block gave brief speeches.[48] The 1975 homecoming saw the Archers defeat Goshen. During half time, Jake McClure, George Collyer, LeRoy Cook and Bill Bower were inducted into the Athletic Hall of Fame. A student dance took place in the cafeteria to the music of "A Taste of Honey." A crowd of nearly 300 was on hand to see Brian Teixeira named king and Debbie Dolby named queen.[49]

On the club scene in the mid 1970's, the old traditional clubs such as Hi-Y headed by Robert Weber, and Philo were still active. The Meterites were still hosting the Quarter Century Banquet. The Afro American Club was one of South Side's most active clubs during the mid 1970's. Under the leadership of President George Ashford, Vice President Kathy Terry, Secretary-Treasurer Pam Elliot and Program Chairman Pam Burns, this club instituted a tradition of giving a Thanksgiving basket to a needy family. In addition, they attended black expositions, held a variety show during the month of March, and participated in a city-wide dance. This club, which was sponsored by Frances Gooden, was also instru-

mental in founding the Pom Pom Girls who became a South Side institution.[50] One of the new clubs at South Side in the 1975-76 school year was the War Games Club sponsored by Mr. Arthur Peffley. The purpose of this club was to recreate military situations. In addition, a new Fishing Club under the direction of Mr. Richard Bussard was formed.[51] The Letterman's Club under the direction of George Robert Davis and the Cinderellas also founded by Mr. Davis were still very active in the mid 70's. The Cinderellas were a group of girls who helped out at track meets.[52] The South Side High School Music Department continued offering strong programs in the mid 1970's. Long-time veteran Robert Drummond approaching three decades of service at South Side headed the department and directed instrumental music. Keith Morphew directed the band and also took over choir directing duties when John Meadows departed for Ball State University.[53]

During the 1974-75 school year, a new dimension was added to the South Side athletic program as the girls varsity basketball team made its debut. Behind the capable coaching of Ella Jones and John

Vista, the girls team experienced an excellent season. They defeated opponents by large margins. The team had a tremendous height advantage and was successful in dominating the boards with the rebounding skills of Laure Harwood and others. Leading scorers on the team included Michelle Irving, Sue Williams and Brenda Byrd. The biggest disappointment for the girls basketball team was that they would

1972 – Archerettes: Jackie Yerger, Sheree Lowden, Jenny Snow, Vicki Keenan, Laurie Rose, Cynthia Adams, Pam Brooks, Lillian Edgar, Denise Marshall, Marsha Muterspaugh.

not be able to take their team toward a state championship because the first IHSAA sanctioned girls state basketball tournament was not scheduled until the 1976 basketball season.[54] The girls varsity basketball team had a very successful season in 1975-76 losing only one game and capturing the SAC championship. The team was again coached by Ella Jones and reached the title game in the sectional losing in overtime. Julie Halgren and Susan Williams were named members of the All Sectional team. Other outstanding individuals from this SAC championship team were Kathy Wright and Brenda Byrd.

During the 1974-75 season, the girls gymnastics team had a winning record and coach Bill Close was elected gymnastics "Man of the Year."[55] The 1975 girls' tennis team finished with a perfect record of 11 wins and no losses winning the SAC crown. Leslie Koehlinger, the number one player, advanced to the regionals where she was beaten by the girl who eventually became the state champion.[56] Other members of this outstanding 1975 girls tennis team were Donna Beck, Chris Myers, Janeen Meyers, Kathy Sprunger and Linda Rose. The year 1975 also marked the first year for girls' varsity track. South Side was destined to dominate the state in the 1980's winning four girls' state track championships and producing numerous individual stars and record setters. The first girls varsity track team in 1975 was coached by Ella Jones. Janice Harris qualified for the state finals.[57]

In boys' sports, the varsity wrestling team, which had been started in the 1960's by Ray Hyde, continued to produce very competitive performers during the mid 1970's. Tim Foster set an individual season record with 23 wins during the 1974 wrestling season and this was matched by Howard Savage in 1975. For his entire career during the mid 1970's, Howard Savage won 57 matches and was a state finalist in 1975. During the 1975 wrestling season, Howard Savage lost only one match. Tim Foster who had performed one year before Howard Savage achieved a brilliant 23-2 record in 1974 and went to the state finals.[58] During the 1975 baseball season, Steve Kurtz batted .431 which was a South Side record.[59] The 1976 varsity baseball team had a very surprising season considering the fact that it had only four returning letterman. The team won a then record 17 games under new head coach Rick Danley. Curt Sery, a junior pitcher won 11 of those games. This team finished as co-champions in the SAC and were runners-up in the sectional.[60] The 1977 baseball team was to achieve even greater heights winning 19 games (a school record) as well as the SAC championship.[61] The 1975 boys' golf team had a fine season winning the SAC championship and finishing with a record of 21-4. In his second year as golf coach, Richard

Karen Azar and Chuck Jackson suit their
dancing styles to each other

Melton produced a great team. Tom Poitras and Mike Johnson were named All SAC.[62] During the 1976 golf season, Mamie McClure was recognized as the first known female golfer in SAC competition. She was actually a member of the boys varsity golf team.[63]

On the football field, Frank Houk replaced Robert Gernand as head football coach in 1974. Robert Gernand in 18 seasons of coaching produced 72 victories. This was exceeded only by the 76 victories won by Coach Lundy Welborn during 14 seasons at the Archer football helm in the 1920's and 30's.[64] Frank Houk produced good Archer football teams during the mid 1970's. The 1974 Archer football squad won five and lost five and represented the south division in the city championship. The 1975 Archer football team won six and lost three. John Arnold was named to All State and All American teams and Carl Geesaman totalled the second highest yards in the city. The following year in 1976, the Archer gridders did even better as they won seven of nine games. Standouts on this football team were running backs Joe Swinford and Greg Hunter. Quarterback Dave Post tossed numerous successful passes to split end Vince Pearson.[65] Murray Mendenhall's Archer basketball team repeated as sectional champions in 1975 but again lost in the regional. In 1976, the Archer basketball team had a successful season but lost in the sectional to Concordia in a double overtime. The 1976-77 basketball team was Murray Mendenhall's finest squad up to that time. This team had a 16-game winning streak, won the sectional championship for the third time in four years, and defeated the state's second ranked team on their way to winning South Side's first regional championship in ten years. In the semi-state tournament, South Side defeated defending state champion, Marion, but then suffered a disappointing four-point loss to Carmel in the semi-state final. Travis McGee and Tom Mendenhall were named to the All Semi-State team.[66]

In the autumn of 1975, South Side graduate and veteran teacher Lois Holtmeyer replaced Mary Edith Reiff as head of the Foreign Language Department. Miss Reiff retired after a quarter century of service. In the mid 1970's, the veterans on the South Side faculty included Robert Drummond, Glenn Stebing and Robert Weber, all of whom had joined the South Side faculty in the late 1940's. The teacher with the longest period of service was Mary Graham who started her South Side teaching career in 1942. Among those teachers who came to South Side in the early 1950's and were still on the staff in the mid 1970's were Jack Weicker and Robert Petty, long-time math teacher. Both Mr. Weicker and Mr. Petty came to South Side in the autumn of 1951.[67] Among the new teachers arriving at South Side in the fall of 1975 was Terry Flynn, later to serve many years as head basketball coach. Joining the South Side staff in the fall of 1975 was

Beverly Henry Wyss. She was a graduate of the South Side class of 1952 and would spend more than 20 years serving as secretary to principals Jack Weicker and Jennifer Manth.[68] South Side traditions continued in the mid 1970's. On the 40th anniversary of Ivy Day in 1976, Alanza Edmonds was chosen Ivy Day Queen.[69]

By the late 1970's, the age of majority had become 18 years not 21 years as it had been for previous generations of young Americans. This new age of majority raised serious questions for South Side's senior students. Questions such as, "Should we continue to live with our parents, or should we rent an apartment and battle inflation by ourselves?" The 1978 *Totem* proclaimed, "We are searching to find ourselves in a world with billions of different faces, personalities and values. Our individual build up is painful and difficult. But growing up was never intended to be an easy ride. Freedom is part of a coin; one side is freedom, the other side is responsibility. We are free to choose how our lives are altered and changed. You can not have one side of the coin without the other."[70] The most widespread fad at South Side High School in the late 1970's was inspired by the popular John Travolta style disco fever. The girls brought out the straight legged pants while the boys stepped into their high fashioned three piece suits.[71] There had also been an evolution with regard to the hangouts popular with South Side students. In the 20's and 30's we had Nick's and the South Side Grill; in the 40's, 50's and 60's, we had Miller's, Hall's and Azar's; in the late 70's, it was McDonald's and Pizza King.[72] In June of 1977, Mary Graham and Laverne Harader retired. Ironically, both Miss Graham and Mr. Harader had graduated from South Side in 1929. Mary Graham who came to South Side in 1942 closed out a 35-year teaching career, while Mr. Harader who joined the faculty in 1955 completed 22 years on the staff.[73]

In the autumn of 1977, Jennifer Manth joined the South Side faculty as an English teacher and became department head following the untimely death of David Cowdrey.[74] In 1990, Jennifer Manth would succeed Jack Weicker as principal of South Side High School. During the 1977-78 school year, four computer terminals were installed in the Math Lab. South Side became one of the many area high schools to share the use of the central computer terminals which were located in the Fort Wayne Community Schools Administration Building. Computer math was a new course offered to all math students. The class operated on an independent study basis in which students worked at their own pace, and if necessary received assistance from the instructor who was Richard Sage, longtime head of the Math Department. To assist students in an ever-changing world where they were "on their own at age 18," the Home Economics Department under Juanita Mendenhall offered various courses on human development, managed housing and single living. The single living course offered to seniors taught students how to get along while living alone. It taught them such things as finding an apartment, budgeting money, and making simple repairs on clothing.[75]

Engineer Archie James rests before he climbs to the highlight of his long day.

In the winter of 1978, South Side students experienced the famous "blizzard of 78." In the autumn of 1978, a new program for sophomores was initiated. They were required to take a nine-week course in speech. Mary Jane Crum and Robert Kelly taught these students. The classes taught the students to read, organize and present material. The purpose was to help students think on their feet, get organized and learn not to be afraid to speak before others. In the autumn of 1978, the Foreign Language Department headed by Lois Holtmeyer offered four languages, French, Spanish, Latin and German. The Art Department offered a variety of highly instructive courses. Mr. Frank Roberts, head of the Art Department, taught photography, arts and crafts. Mr. George Robert Davis, a chemistry teacher, heartlessly commented, "Weekends were made for chemistry." The Science Department offered a variety of useful courses. Two basic courses, Applied Life and Applied Physical Science helped students to understand every day occurrences of life. These were taught by Robert Weber and David Griggs. Earth Science, a class designated to deal with geography and astronomy was instructed by Gary Black while Richard Bussard taught physics. At this time, the Music Department was still presided over by Robert Drummond. The choir director was Keith Morphew and the new band director was Earl Jackson. The social studies department studied current events and took trips to the Museum of Science and Industry in Chicago. William Hedges, head of the department said, "We set our goals to get students interested and involved in their government, and they responded well." In physical education classes, students enjoyed softball, archery, bowling, volleyball, tennis and track. With the disco craze hitting South Side, students had fun learning how to boogie in dance class. There was also a body building class. The dance class was taught by Ella Jones and the other physical education teachers were Walter Bartkiewicz, Glenn Stebing and a new teacher Roberta Widmann (later Roberta Widmann-Foust) who was to build the dramatically successful girls track program at South Side beginning in the late 1970's which produced four state track championships in the 1980's.[76]

On the gridiron, Coach Frank Houk continued to produce winning teams in the late 1970's. Standout Archer football players of this era included Byron Hunter, Bob Tyree, Adrian White, Craig Willis, Ivory Turner, Ken Fowlkes, Jeff Benson and Vernon Martin. On the basketball court, Murray Mendenhall's team won sectional titles in 1978 and 1979 but were eliminated both years in the regional. In seven seasons of coaching, Mendenhall's teams had won five sectional titles."[77] Outstanding Archer basketball players of the late 1970's included Tom Mendenhall, Lance Brown, Jim Singleton, Earl Dunson, Ron Tabron, Keith Gilbert, and one of the most effective players ever to wear the Archer uniform, John Flowers. Coach Bill Walker continued to field superb boys track teams in the late 1970's. The 1977 team finished fourth at the state finals. Archers finishing second in their events at the state meet were Leon Tubbs in the 440, Bob Tyree in the high jump and the 880 relay team consisting of Leon Tubbs, Craig Willis, Karl Kelsaw and Ed Nolan. This team scored 40 points at the state finals. The 1978 boys track team did even better finishing second at the state finals, and in 1979, the boys track team posted an undefeated season. The period of the late 70's was perhaps the golden age of boys track at South Side High School featuring many outstanding individuals who broke virtually all of the existing school track records. Outstanding among these were Leon Tubbs and Ron Birchfield who set state and national records. In 1978, six Archer track men went to the state competition including Robert Tyree, Leon Tubbs, Jeff Benson, Glen Windom, Mark O'Shaughnessy and Karl Kelso. Leon Tubbs set a state record in winning the 440 yard dash at the 1978 state track finals. In 1979, Ron Birchfield won the first of his two consecutive state championships in the 300 meter hurdles.[78] In the late 1970's, the boys tennis teams under coach Jim Tarr were highly successful. In 1977 and 1978, Steve LaMar lost only one match before moving to California. During the period of the late 1970's, Tom Lazoff achieved the unbelievable record of winning 44 consecutive singles matches without a defeat. Tom Lazoff stands with Dick Doermer and Paul Dammeyer of the late 30's and early 40's as the greatest Archer tennis players of all time.[79]

In 1978, Roberta Widmann, who was to build nationally recognized girls track program at South Side, coached her first squad which won 10 meets out of 11. This 1978 girls track team won the SAC meet, the sectionals and the regionals.[80] In 1979, the girls track team under the direction of Coach Widmann experienced an undefeated season winning the SAC meet and the sectional title.[81] This outstanding team finished second at the state meet. The South Side girls 800 yard medley relay team made up of Lisa Roehm, Pat Tibbs, Jill Myers, and Robin Beasley won first place at the state meet. This 1979 girls track team also produced South Side's first female track superstar Delores Stewart. At one time, she held school records in the 100, 220, and 440 yard runs. At the state track meet in 1979, she won the 440 yard dash and finished third in the 220. Other outstanding individuals on this 1979 girls track team included Teresa Smethers, Yolanda Benson and Chris Kolkman.[82]

By 1979, the prom had become a junior-senior affair and was held at the IPFW Ballroom.[83] In 1979, the Ivy Day tradition was very much alive at South Side as the school celebrated its 44th Ivy Day. The class of 1979 took their final march in front of the school. The parade concluded in the east parking lot of the school where the entire senior class went on to the Ivy Day ceremony in the auditorium. Jeff Presley spoke briefly and effectively on what being at South had meant to him and what effects South Side would have on his life in the future. Mark Clevenger, senior class president, gave a speech on the meaning of Ivy Day and the highlight of the ceremony was the crowing of the Ivy Day Queen, Katy Keenan. The Ivy Day court consisted of Concetta Walker, Linda Spenny, Amy McClure, Cindy Wyss, Carla Hunter and Nora Kowal.[84] At the end of the 1970's, South Side was still experiencing high academic achievement. On recognition night held June 3, 1979, over 100 students were given awards for excellence in academics. In the recognition night procession, the valedictorian of the class of 1979 James Buuck was followed by salutatorian Kevin Leamon. South Side scholars were Becky Haffner, John Buuck, Tom Matson, John Martin, Lori Benninghoff, Linda Spenny, Becky Anderson, Laura Houser and Cindy Cobbs. Among the recipients of other awards at the 1979 Recognition Night was Shiroz Keshwani who was the top sophomore winning the coveted R. Nelson Snider Award. In addition, 81 seniors of the class of 1979 were elected to the National Honor Society.[85]

When school opened in the fall of 1979, South Side once again had a freshmen class after an absence of many years. The school was again a four-year high school.[86] Many new teachers were required due to the presence once again of a freshmen class. Among the new teachers in the autumn of 1979 were Martin Erickson, a 1969 graduate, and Joan Hattendorf Varketta, a 1955 graduate. As a sign of the times and with ever increasing emphasis on security, Donald Hoover, a Fort Wayne City policeman, was employed full time at South Side High School.[87] As the 1970's ended, veteran teachers still on the faculty were Robert Drummond and Glen Stebing, both of whom had started their teaching careers at South Side in 1947, Robert Weber who came to South Side in 1948, and Jack Weicker and Robert Petty, both of whom had joined the South Side faculty in 1951.

Phil Pranger takes a rare break from car-hopping
at the "beer" stand

The 1985 Girl's State Champions wave to
their loyal supporters during the Three Rivers Parade.
/photo by Watters

CHAPTER SEVEN
1980-1989

A. Girls' State Track Champions — Four Times

As the 1980's began, gasoline topped one dollar per gallon for the first time. Downtown revital-ization in Fort Wayne was a prime topic of conversation, and rock concerts made a welcomed comeback a the Coliseum. There were more drug and pornography raids throughout the city while strikes at Harvester and Dana and layoffs at Zollner added to the concern on the Fort Wayne labor front. On the national scene, the Soviet Union had invaded Afghanistan and there was a suggestion that the United States might boycott the 1980 summer Olympics being held in Moscow.[1] At South Side High School, the autumn of 1980, saw a drop in enrollment from the 1,770 students of the previous year to 1,580.[2] In the halls of South Side, fashions definitely featured the "preppy" look. Students were wearing the type of clothing that their parents had worn in high school. Girls were into oxford cloth skirts with button down collars. Pleated skirts had made a comeback. The perm was out and most girls were reverting back to the feathered look or trying braids. The boys at South Side were also into the "preppy" look. They wore casu-al pants and a preppy shirt. Long hair had also come back into style. Musical bands such as "Blondie," "The Cars," and "Devo" had all gained quick popularity with new wave fans. Disco which had swept the country with such great force in the mid and late 70's still played a major role in the music world despite its declining popularity. Hard rock, especially from bands that featured a southern style remained a favorite with many music lovers. For the true music lover, attending a concert seemed the ultimate goal. This goal became reachable as such groups as "The Commodores," "Molly Hatchet," and "The Charlie

1980 State Champion Girls Track Team
Front row: Jackson, Tibbs, Benson, Smikth, Arnold, Myers, Morris, Temple.
Second row: Beasley, Mendez, Tubbs, Auld Pietzak, Sykes, Brand.
Third row: Coach Widmann, Young, Tyler, Hollins, Roehm, C. Kolkman, M. Koikman, Thompson.
Back row: Coach Davis, Coach Erickson, C. Tyree, Flowers, G. Tyree, Smethers, Gatewood.

Daniels Band" performed at the Coliseum.[3] The year 1980 also saw the introduction of various electronic games which could either be hand held or played with the aid of television.[4]

At Recognition Day in 1980, Rob Manges was given the award for being valedictorian with an average of 98%. Jenny Langhinrichs was named salutatorian. Her average was 97.94%. Five other seniors with averages of 95% or better were named as "South Side Scholars." These five individuals were Julie Athan, Arthur Fogel, Thomas Gidley, Teresa Hughes and Carol Hummel.[5] In 1980, a unique and unusual course of study known as the Lau Program was instituted by veteran teacher Janet Perez. This program was necessitated due to an increase in the number of Asian students enrolled at South Side. During the early stages of the program, there were 23 students, 17 of whom came from Laos. As the first semester began, the average length of time that each student had been in the United States was only five months. The students were taught not only English but mathematics, social studies and American culture. By December of 1980, many of these students had been main streamed into regular South Side classes.[6] The Music Department was still under the direction of Robert Drummond who had been a faculty member since 1947. In the autumn of 1981, the South Side marching band ("The Marching Green Machine") under new director David Streeter won the division title and a trip to the state finals. This was the first time that a South Side marching band had ever gone to the state finals. The Majorettes, an organization with long tradition at South Side, were still firmly in place under the direction of senior Natalie Nunez.[7] In the early 1980's, the Afro American Club was South Side's largest organization. Boasting a membership of 158, the club was one of the school's most active organizations, sponsoring an exciting talent and fashion show in the spring in which more than 200 students participated.[8] Other clubs still going strong in the early 1980's were Philo, sponsoring the Powder Puff football game, and Hi-Y, still under the sponsorship of Robert Weber. The Social Studies Club started an investment club headed by Mr. William Hedges. This club gave students the opportunity to invest in stock and then share in the profits or losses.[9] The French Club was rejuvenated by veteran teacher Dorothy Wynn.[10] In the early 80's, Anne White was still director of publications, and South Side could still be proud of a superior yearbook under the direction of such *Totem* editors as Mike Wilkens, Patty Ashman and Karen Gemmer.[11] The *South Side Times* continued to flourish under the leadership of such editors as Bobby Hutner, Bob Toy, John Gevers and Laura Feidler, and with clever and imaginative photographs by John Sanderson and Todd Anderson.[12]

1981 Featured Alumnus - Miss Helne Foellinger, News-Sentinel publisher, sits at her desk, trying to get caught up on some "paper" work.

South Side High School athletics in the early 1980's were dominated by boys basketball and girls and boys track. Pres Brown, long-time South Side athletic director, commenting on the 1979-80 boys basketball team stated that this team possessed possibly the greatest array of talent that he had ever seen.[13] This team, coached by Murray Mendenhall and featuring such talented players as John Flowers, Ron Tabron, Keith Gilbert, Scottie Ferrell, Mike Cunningham and Irvin Hairston won the sectional and regional titles. In the first game of the semi-state tournament, they defeated Valparaiso in a triple overtime. Unfortunately, the team ran out of gas after this Herculean effort and was defeated in the semi-state final by

Marion.[14] John Flowers, one of South Side's great basketball players, became the third Archer to score more than 1,000 points in his career. He graduated in 1981 and was named to several All State and All American teams. At the conclusion of the 1980-81 basketball season, Murray Mendenhall retired as South Side's coach. Mr. Mendenhall had been head boys basketball coach for nine seasons. During that period, his teams won six sectional and two regional championships. In girls track, Roberta Widmann, who had assumed the coaching reigns in 1978, succeeded in building a nationally recognized program. In 1980, the South Side girls track team won the state track title. This was the first of four state championships to be won by the Archer girls track team in the 1980's. Members of the 1980 state championship team included Gloria Tyree, Lisa Roem, Chris Kolkman, Robin Beasley, Yolanda Benson, Patricia Tibbs, Trina Flowers, Cathey Tyree, Jill Myers and Theresa Temple. Freshman Cathey Tyree was the team's only individual state champion placing first in the high jump. The 880 yard medley relay team consisting of Lisa Roem, Patricia Tibbs, Theresa Temple and Jill Myers, also placed first at state. This 1980 state champion girls track team was undefeated during the regular season making it the second consecutive undefeated season achieved by the girls track team. From 1978 through 1981, the girls track team won 25 consecutive meets.[15]

The 1980 boys track team under the coaching of Bill Walker completed its second consecutive undefeated season. They won the sectional and regional by very large margins, and finished second at the 1980 state meet. Individual records were set at the 1980 state track meet by Ron Birchfield who won the 300 meter hurdles and by Lee Wilson who garnered a first place in the discus. Ron Birchfield's time in the 300 meter hurdles was the nation's best, thus making him an All American at this event. The boys 400 meter relay team consisting of Charles Pullard, Jesse Wims, John Flowers, and Phil Birchfield set a school record while placing second at the state meet. The 1600 meter relay team consisting of Bobby Williams,

1980 Semi-State Runners-up
First Row - Ron Mayers, Charles J. Fanning, Rob Brink, Bill Chavis, Mike Cunningham, Scott Ferrell, Ken Helvie;
second row - Mr. Murray Mendenhall, Wallace Jordan, John Flowers, Keith Gilbert, Irv Hairston, Ron Tabron, Mr. Terry Flynn

Jeff Jackson, Ron Birchfield and Phil Birchfield likewise set a school record at the state meet. Other outstanding individuals on the boys 1980 boys track team were Ron Tabron, Rodney Davis and Robert Davis.[16] In 1981, the boys track team had another outstanding season. For the second consecutive year, they were runners-up at the state track meet. Ron Birchfield repeated his performance by winning his second consecutive state championship in the 300 meter hurdles. He set a state record and was again named to the high school All American track team. Archer football teams of the early 1980's were coached by Frank Houk who was replaced by John Hester at the beginning of the 1983 season.[17] The 1981 Archer football team received honorable mention in the state rankings. This team defeated North Side for the first time in seven years as quarterback Tim Manges scored in the final seconds. Phil Birchfield finished first in city rushing in 1981, and Tim Manges was second in passing.[18]

In the early 1980's, some of the so-called minor sports at South Side continued to gain attention. The 1980 boys tennis team was coached by

After winning several important events, Ron Birchfield, senior, demonstrates one of his unique styles by running a leg in the 440 relay.

South Side graduate LeeAnn Berning. She became the first woman ever to coach a boys tennis team in the city of Fort Wayne.

The 1981 and 1982 boys tennis teams were coached by Rick Hannauer, and won the SAC championship in both years. The 1981 boys tennis team won South Side's first sectional in history. This 1981

John Flowers slams home another dunk against SAC opponent Snider.

varsity tennis team consisted of Brad Fenner, John Colvin, Doug Rowe, Jim Richardson, Ed Minnich, Chris Miller and C.J Graf.[19] The 1981 and 1982 South Side baseball teams coached by Dean Doerffler won a total of 31 games. The 1981 team called the greatest in South Side history by Coach Doerffler featured such players as Pete Weaver, Shannon Stanfield and Ray Young, all of whom were named to the All City team. Jeff Trammel won the batting title with an average of .444 before a late season injury marked the end of his season. Bret Pippin was named to the Second All City team.

In March of 1982, the worst flood since 1913 ravaged the city of Fort Wayne. One-third of the city's population fought the rising waters by placing sand bags. Two-thirds of these were teenagers with a large number from South Side High School. President Ronald Reagan even came to town to help throw sand bags as Mayor Win Moses, a South Side graduate, called for teenagers to help fight the flood. Fort Wayne received national attention from the flood which created damage estimated at $28 million. Ann Landers dedicated her famous news column to the "Youth that Saved a City."[20] The early 1980's marked the retirement of another longtime South Side faculty member as Robert Petty concluded his teaching service in June of 1982. Mr. Petty had started his South Side career in 1951. South Side's link with the 1940's was still preserved through 1982 as Robert Drummond, Glenn Stebing, and Robert Weber, all of whom had joined the faculty in the late 1940's, remained. [21] The early 1980's also witnessed the conclusion of the career of perhaps the greatest female basketball player thus far in the history of South Side High School. In 1983, Cathey Tyree graduated holding career records in points scored and rebounds as well as season records in points scored and rebounds. She was named an Indiana All Star and was named to the 1983 All State girls basketball team.[22] Cathey Tyree joined Delores Stewart and a future standout DeDe Nathan as being among the greatest female athletes in South Side High School history. In 1983, South Side graduate Win Moses was elected to his second four-year term as mayor of Fort Wayne. In the same year, Bob Sievers, South Side graduate and long-time WOWO radio personality, was approaching his 50th year on the air. On the national scene, President Reagan signed into law the creation of a national holiday honoring Martin Luther King, Jr., and a "Chorus Line" became the longest running broadway play.[23] The year 1983 was also a year of change at South Side High School. Retiring in 1983 as head of the Music Department was Robert Drummond who concluded a 36-year career at South Side. Pres Brown and Richard Block joined the Quarter Century Club and McDonald's moved from its Calhoun Street location to Rudisill Boulevard.[24] New computers were installed and some remodeling was done to accommodate them. "South Side Pride" summed up South's new feeling. This phrase was painted on the walls by the cafeteria and the gym.[25] By 1983, it was possible for South Side students to take advantage of certain courses offered at the Regional Vocational School (the old Central High School). RVS offered such programs as child care, data programming, beauty culture, automotive and many others. The director of RVS at South was Jennifer Manth.[26]

The Home Economics Department under Juanita Mendenhall continued to offer the popular Human Development course which was set up to help students become more aware of life as a parent and what it takes to manage a home and a family. The English Department was in the process of making a transition that would allow American Literature and American History to be studied at the same time. The Foreign Language Department under the direction of Lois Holtmeyer offered four years of study in French, Latin, German and Spanish. A fifth year independent study course was offered for students who had finished four years in Spanish or French. The Math Department under the leadership of Richard Sage was featuring a class in computer math. Mr. Sage summed up the climate at South Side in the mid 1980's when he stated, "We are in a time of great transition. The future is going to be for those who are able to adapt to the rapid changes taking place in

Over the hurdle flies DeDe Nathan, junior, on her way to a 2nd consecutive state title.

photo by Stearns

every aspect of our society."[27] In the Music Department, Keith Morphew had taken over the concert choir while the freshmen choir was directed by David Streeter. The Marching Green Machine appeared in the Three Rivers Festival Parade and for the second time in three years under the direction of David Streeter achieved a Division 1 rating a the district competition held in October of 1983.[28] The senior class play in 1983 was "The Pink Panther Strikes Again" with leading roles being taken by Dan Bromley, Shelly Anglin and Andy Hufford. The 1983-84 speech season was a rebuilding year as the team was led by Robert Kelly beginning his twelfth year of coaching speech at South Side.[29] On the social scene, the formal dances, of course, had been moved out of the South Side gymnasium and took place at several venues in the mid 1980's. The big spring formal dance was the combined Junior-Senior Prom which was held at such locations as the IPFW Ballroom, the lobby of the Embassy Theater and the Botanical Gardens.[30] On prom night in 1983, the lighted Embassy marquee proclaimed "South Side High School 1983 Prom, a Night on Broadway." The spring talent shows presented by the Afro American Club continued to be smash hits. In 1983, the show was entitled, "Alice in Dreamland." The leading roles belonged to Stacy Files and Brian Johnson, both juniors. In 1985, a show entitled, "Soul Review" was presented with Carolyn Dowdell and Eric Green taking the lead roles. Karen Nichols, president of the club and Steve Tate, vice president, spent their entire summer vacation writing the show. Instrumental in the staging of this outstanding performance was club sponsor Barbara Davis.[31]

By the mid 1980's, there were many third generation students enrolled at South Side High School. A junior, Todd Morley, summed up the feeling when he said, "My grandparents went to this school and sent their children to South Side. Naturally, I'm here."[32] Even though the mid 80's were periods of change and transition at South Side High School, the old traditions continued to be honored. The annual Queen of Hearts Dance sponsored by Hi-Y was celebrating its fourth decade. In 1985, Faith Worthman was elected Queen of Hearts and was escorted to her throne by Hi-Y president Russell

1980 - Afro American Club

Kolkman.[33] Spirit Days were still going strong in 1985 and included such days as "Nerd Day," "College Sweats Day," "Funeral Day," "Hawaiian Shirt Day," "Crazy Green and White Day," and "Sunglasses and Hat Day."[34] Another South Side tradition, Ivy Day, continued to be celebrated during the mid 1980's. The 1983 Ivy Day was somewhat unusual since the Queen and all members of her court were senior class officers. The only non-female class officer Phil GiaQuinta (class treasurer) presented the Ivy Day crown to Kris Kurtz. The members of the court were class president Bonita Johnson, Sara Miller, Cina Tuesca, Patti Leamon and Karen Gemmer.[35] Rebecca Schaab reigned as Ivy Day Queen in 1984 while Robbie Sinninger crowned Faith Worthman as South Side's 50th Ivy Day Queen in 1985.[36] As the sign of the times, a new club sponsored by Mr. Frank Houk appeared in the autumn of 1984. This new club was Students Against Drunk Driving.[37]

Anne White and Mike Wilkins

The mid 1980's continued to be good years for the South Side High School publications. In 1984, Anne White retired after 21 years as head of the Archer publications. She was replaced by Douglas Laslie who would guide the Times, Totem and other South Side publications for the next 12 years.[38] The Totem under such editors as Shelly Davis, Jennifer Graham and Kim Plasterer continued to be a superb yearbook. The South Side Times under the leadership of such editors as Tom Manges and Mark Clark continued its tradition as one of the country's fine high school newspapers. In 1985, a literary publication entitled, "*Inklings*" made its debut. "*Inklings*" was a worthy successor to "*Pegasus*" which had been South Side's literary magazine in the 1960's.[39] Highlighting the academic awards in the mid 1980's were 1985 South Side scholars Ernest Stainaker (valedictorian), Scott Morris (salutatorian), Jerry Gerig, Nora Mills, Amy Simon and Eric Zimmerman.[40]

The mid 1980's saw the usual array of retirements and shifts in the faculty. In 1984, long-time custodial engineer Archie James was given a 30-year certificate by superintendent Bill Anthis. Included among the additions to the faculty in the early to mid 80's were Francis Mustapha, Kathy Kerbel and Christine Shafer.[41] In the autumn of 1983, the new Archer football coach was John Hester who took the place of Frank Houk. Mr. Houk became assistant to the principal. By the autumn of 1985, the administrative staff consisted of Jack Weicker, principal, Richard Block, assistant principal and Jennifer Manth, Francis Gooden, Thomas Gordon, and William Hedges as assistants to the principal. Notable faculty retirements in the mid 1980's were, as mentioned, Robert Drummond in 1983 and Glenn Stebing in 1985. Mr. Stebing, former varsity basketball coach, had also taught driver's training, served as assistant coach in various sports, and headed the intramural and physical education departments during his 38 years of service at South Side High School. By the autumn of 1985, only one teacher who was on the faculty in the 1940's remained at South Side. This was Robert Weber who started his teaching career at South Side in 1948. Other faculty veterans still on the staff in 1985 were Principal Jack Weicker who started his South

1982 - Lau Club

Side teaching career in 1951, and Robert Gernand who joined the faculty in 1954.

The sports scene at South Side during the middle 1980's was dominated by the excellence of the girls track program established by Roberta Widmann. After winning the state championship in 1980, Coach Widmann's teams went through two rebuilding seasons in the early 1980's before winning the sectionals and finishing fifth at the 1983 state meet. The 1983 team was made up primarily of freshmen. One of these freshmen was DeDe Nathan who many believe to be South Side's greatest individual female track performer. At the 1983 state track meet, the 1600 meter relay team made up of freshmen Trudy McCloud, DeDe Nathan, and Angie Goodman, along with senior standout Cathey Tyree finished first breaking the state record.[42] In 1984, the South Side girls track team finished second at the state meet with DeDe Nathan winning the state title in the 300 meter low hurdles. The South Side girls repeated as champions in the 1600 meter relay with a team consisting of Lisa Martin, Angie Goodman, Trudy McCloud and DeDe Nathan.[43] The 1985 Archer girls track team won first place in the sectionals, regionals and won South Side's second girls state title. This championship team consisted of DeDe Nathan, Trudy McCloud, Cori Kelso, Anita Mendez and Janet Hayden. At the state meet, DeDe Nathan won the 100 and 300 meter hurdles and placed fourth in the long jump. She set two state records and three school records.[44] The 1986 girls track team went through the entire season undefeated winning the sectional and regional titles and repeating as state track champions. According to Coach Roberta Widmann, "Three of the most talented women athletes to graduate from South" in the person of Trudy McCloud, DeDe Nathan and Cori Kelso led this team.[45]

Despite being overshadowed by the miraculous accomplishments of the girls track team, there were other bright moments in Archer athletics in the mid 1980's. The 1983 boys tennis team, even though hit heavily by graduation, finished second in the SAC. This team was made up of Chris Sanderson, Tom Manges, Todd Anderson, Jerry Gerig, Dan Bromley and Joe Deitche. The 1983 Archer golf team under Coach Richard Melton finished 19 and 4 and tied for the SAC championship. This team was made up of Scott Hull, John Didier, Rich Deister, Pete Gemmer and Todd Anderson. The 1984 boys baseball team coached by David Fireoved won 15 games. They were runners-up in the sectional losing to Northrop. The team was led by three All City players, Jeff Dawson, Mike Preston and James Gilbert. [46] South Side's boys basketball teams under Coach Terry Flynn produced winning records in the mid 1980's but had tough luck in the sectional tournament suffering one point losses to Northrop and Harding in 1984 and 1985 respectively. Among the outstanding Archer basketball players of this period were Ed Starks, Todd Starks, George Baldus, Reggie Grady, Ron Keller and Gent Montgomery.

Principal Jack Weicker contemplates the future.

B. Athens in Ruins?

In 1986, Jack Weicker was beginning his 24th year as principal of South Side High School. By 1986, parts of South Side were in serious need of renovation and updating. There had been some changes in the neighborhood and all of these factors prompted some to think that South Side High School had seen its best days. Thanks to the inspired guidance of Mr. Weicker, a fine administrative staff, an excellent faculty and a student body who boasted academic excellence and cultural diversity, South Side High School worked to dispel the notion that Athens was in ruins. In 1986, Jack Weicker was named "Indiana Administrator of the Year" by the state's Association of Educational Secretaries. He was nominated for this award by Beverly Henry Wyss, his secretary. In commenting on the educational atmosphere that existed in the mid to late 1980's, Jack Weicker stated, "I'm fond of saying if all the innovative educators who had been operating for the past 25 years were laid end to end, they would reach from here to the moon and in that position would do a tremendously less amount of damage than they did here on earth. We believe in young people and we believe that tomorrow will be better than today...so it becomes imperative that we do all we can while we have them (the South Side students) and that has been the philosophy of this high school since 1922. There is something special about South Side High School that keeps faculty and staff here. I've never had any desire to leave this building and go anywhere else and I'm not alone."[47]

Among the new teachers joining the faculty in the autumn of 1986 were Greg Taylor and David Brumm, both South Side graduates. The 1986 South Side varsity football team was the best in several

1982 - Speech Team

years winning five games and losing three during the regular season. The offense was led by Carlton Mabel and Tim Gaskill while the running attack was led by Tony Easly and All SAC back Shane Younker.[48] The 1987 varsity football team had a winning season and went all the way to the sectional championship before losing. Seniors Terry Reese, Keith Nathan and junior Adrian Mabel were named to the first team All City squad.[49] In the Media Center, many exciting changes were made under the direction of Dr. Anne Spann and Kathy Kerbel. In the Speech Department, still headed by Robert Kelly, Craig Chambers received the Outstanding Speaker Award while Brian Bolton and Mike Rogers were presented a Performing Arts trophy. Margaret Norton earned the Elizabeth Ann Bromley Award and Holly Hunter received the Stage Struck Award. In the mid 1980's, an Archer Pride Corps made up of pom-pom girls was organized to supplement the Marching Green Machine. There were 28 girls in the pom-pom corp, and the first four girls to respond, who later became captains of the squad, were Kelly Murphy, Kris Buck, Nicole Storry and Mary Bailey.[50]

On the club scene, the Rifle Club was still going strong after forty years and the Afro American Club under the direction of Barbara Davis was still one of South Side's leading organizations. Philo was in its seventh decade as a South Side club and was still sponsoring the Powder Puff football game. A new club in the mid 1980's was the "Archer Hospitality Crew." This club was sponsored by Mrs. Jean Lorraine and Mrs. Francis Gooden and its purpose was to welcome new students in their difficult transition from another school. The Wrestlerettes also emerged in the mid 1980's, and they were a rejuvenation of the Matt Maids. Project Lead sponsored by Sandy Zalas was another new club in the mid 1980's.[51] Perhaps the most notable new addition to South Side's clubs in the mid 1980's was its academic team. In 1986-87, the team coached by Robert Kelly won the state championship in the area of science and placed third in the state in both English and allaround categories. The winning science team was made up of Chris Lamont, Matt Elliott and Avonna Grill.[52]

In the spring of 1987, the tradition of the spring musical was revived as the curtain went up on the newly written musical production entitled, "Funky Winkerbean's Homecoming." South Side became one of the first schools in the nation to produce this musical. It was based on the nationally syndicated comic strip,

"Funky Winkerbean" and the musical dealt with the activities that took place at Westview High during the week before the homecoming game. Starring in the production were Paul Boyer as the outcast nerd, Les Moore who later becomes the school hero and Debbi Thatcher as the airheaded majorette Holly Bud. The director of this musical was Lois Holtmeyer and she was assisted musically by David Streeter and Christine Shafer. The Afro American Club presented its Sole Review in the spring of 1987. The Sole Review was written by the president of the Afro American Club LaDonna Wattley. It was a play in three acts which combined not only drama and music but also a display of current fashions.[53] In the spring of 1988, the senior class organized a totally unofficial and very illegal day known as "Senior Skip Day." Despite its illegality, the school was a lot quieter and the senior locker hall was nearly empty. In 1987, South Side boasted that it was the last public walk-in school in the city.[54] As was stated eloquently by the staff of the *Totem*, judgments about South Side High School in the late 1980's were made by people who had never experienced the Archer way of life. South Side was not a warring ground as many people thought, but rather it was the common ground between many groups of friends. What South Side's 1,300 students lacked in numbers, they more than made up in diversity of people who walked the Archer halls. In these halls were all social classes, religions and races coming together as Archers. They went to games, they went to parties, they learned and they loved together. Spirit and pride became the dominant themes, both on the field and in school. Classrooms were often packed to capacity during club meetings and to look at a South Side crowd during a game was to see nothing but a sea of green. Andrea Muirragui summed it up quite well in the *Totem* when she stated, "South Side is indeed the home of a large Archer family. Like any family, we have problems but we also work together to solve them. We as a whole, the faculty, and the students have worked hard to make South livable, a place to work as well as a place to have fun, a place where difficulties happen, a place where the solutions are found despite what the predetermined beliefs may be."[55]

C. The School That Saved Itself

As the decade of the 1980's was drawing to a close, the 1950's rebel James Dean was back in style and could be seen on everything from full-size posters to pictures on T-shirts. The legend of Marilyn Monroe also made a comeback. Television dance programs became a craze. The classic "American Bandstand" was still around but new productions such as "Dance Party U.S.A." were added. Blue jeans, of course, were still in style but the acid stone washed look and the ripped jean look replaced some of the more conservative styles of the past. Worn out clothes seemed to be the trend. Anything in the brand names of "Banana Republic," "Adidas," "Troop," "Liz Claiborne," "Outback Red," or "Forenza" were in fashion. Michael Jackson's album entitled, "Bad" which was a follow-up to "Thriller" and Bruce Springsteen's albums were the musical hits of the time.[56] At the annual Quill and Scroll Banquet held in the

Yasothala Mahasena masters the computer.

Miss Jennifer Manth, junior class counselor, refers back to past records while trying to help a student with a schedule.

"We're #1," say Angie Goodman, junior, Trucilla McCloud and "DeDe Nathan, freshmen, and Cathey Tyree, senior, after breaking the state record in the 1600-meter relay in 1983.

1983 - Marching Band

spring of 1988, journalism advisor Doug Laslie presented various plaques and trophies. The co-recipients of the Park D. Williams Incentive Award were junior David Snavely and senior Jim Catlin. Junior Shawn Dunahue won the photographer's trophy and the writing trophy was given to Buffy Newton and Elbin Starks, III. In the South Side neighborhood, the old Sears building was revitalized and the acre surrounding the building also underwent a face lift. The summer of 1988 saw one of the worst droughts ever experienced in the city of Fort Wayne. In the autumn of that year, George Bush was elected president and Dan Quayle vice president. The Christmas season of 1988 was marred by the disaster of Pan Am Flight 103 which was blown up by saboteurs.[57]

In the late 1980's, the Archer football program under coach John Hester continued to produce strong competitive teams but the sectional title always seemed to elude them. Outstanding Archer football players of the late 1980's include Juan Gorman, Willy Madison, Elgin Reese and LaMar Smith who went on to play with the Seattle Seahawks of the National Football League.[58] In track, senior Todd Kabisch finished third in the state in the pole vault in 1988 and later finished seventh in a national meet held in Utah. The sports scene at South Side saw the return to dominance of the girls' track program under coach Roberta Widmann-Foust.[59] The 1988 girls' track team finished second at the state meet, and in 1989 the girls' track team won the state championship, their fourth state title in the 1980's. State titles were won by the girls' 400 meter relay team made up of Zanzy Moore, Kiwanna Johnson, Stephanie Wattley and Lynnette Harris. Likewise, the 1600-meter relay team made up of Zanzy Moore, Kiwanna Johnson, Shalonda Davenport and Layette Harris won first place.[60] Also in 1989, Leonard Sweeney shot a school record 34 for a nine-hole round at Foster Park.[61]

In the late 1980's, a public opinion pole was taken among the students who voted that the thing they would most like to change about South Side High School would be to create an open lunch period where students could leave the building. The favorite place to have the South Side High School Prom was the Botanical Gardens and the most preferred restaurant was McDonald's. The favorite teacher of the seniors was Mrs. Phyllis Bush of the English Department.[62] During this same period, South Side's literary magazine entitled, "*Gallery*" took advantage of the new MacIntosh desk top publishing system. The magazine was headed by senior editor Christopher Murray. In 1989, the spring musical was "Anything Goes" and junior Cathy Carlin played the lead. At the annual Quill and Scroll Banquet held in May of 1989, the speaker was Larry Hayes, Opinion Page editor of the *Journal Gazette* and a 1956 graduate of South Side High School. As the decade of the 80's closed, South Side continued its celebration of Ivy Day by crowning Thuy Ngo as 1989 Ivy Queen. Her court consisted of Layette Harris, Dartanya Key, Erin Kohne, Dawn McGuire, Zanzy Moore and Julie Sprague. At Recognition Day in 1989, seniors with an accumulated average of 95% of higher were honored as South Side scholars. The four who accomplished this were Heather Porter (valedictorian), Donna Garringer (salutatorian), Jim Catlin and DaLana Neal. At the Junior-Senior Prom held May 12, 1989, at the Botanical Conservatory, sleet and 42 degree weather did not keep anyone from enjoying "Moonlight Masquerade." During the summer of 1989, the smokestack which had soared high into the sky adjacent to South Side High School since the opening of the school in 1922 was torn down.[63]

As students returned to South Side High School in the late summer of 1989, great changes were in the air. Typewriters had been placed by computers and English class themes and papers began to come straight off the printer. Teachers used computers for anything they had to do for class as they found them as simple as students did. A new concept for many was the use of computers in helping to determine grades. Computers were not the only thing new in the late summer of 1989. As the students returned to school, many wondered if this would be the last year for South Side High School. During the fall of 1989, Section K, the South Side Spirit Club, was revived by Mrs. Renee Albright. At all home basketball games, Archers showed their pride by wearing the colorful Section K t-shirts. Another club new to the school in the 1989-90 school year was the Alpha and Omega Club. Ronnie Latham was elected president of this club, and Jimmie Coleman was vice president.[64]

1987 - Soul Revue Dancers, Jim Kendricks, sophomore, Brent Underwood and Weldon Townsend, juniors, display their best moves to the audience.

photo by Watters

In November of 1989, the Fort Wayne Community Schools Administration unveiled a plan reorganizing the flow of students and converting South Side High School into a grade 6 through 12 magnet school. The entire South Side family, including alumni and neighborhood residents, was mobilized to save the school. Green and white bumper stickers were distributed by a parents group which called itself, "The Friends of South Side." This group passed out green and white bumper stickers which said, "South Side High School…a Fort Wayne Tradition." "Friends of South Side" co-president Brenda Porter stated that the Fort Wayne Community Schools plan affecting South Side High School was not acceptable. Principal Jack Weicker as always the eloquent spokesman for South Side stated, "The faculty has been very successful in educating thousands of students from every walk of life. South Side has a long and distinguished tradition of working with young people…this school prepares people for life because just about everyone is represented here. We try to bring out the best in all of our students."[65] Jack Weicker had previously stated, "South Side's greatest strength in my judgment is that this school has always stressed the worth of the individual. Every student is worthy of the best efforts of this faculty whether he or she be rich or poor, majority or minority, Catholic, Protestant, or Jew. Further, this sense of worth of each individual has kindled a spirit of family in this building that is second to none."[66]

The school proposal did not kill the adamant, passionate spirit which was running through the building at South Side High School. Many students and faculty, whites and blacks, Jews and gentiles, rich and poor and young and old indicated to *Frost Illustrated* that they would not be moved from their beloved institution without just cause.[67] Efforts to turn South Side High School into a magnet school in the late 1980's were thwarted by the tremendous effort of administration, faculty, staff, students, alumni, neighbors, community leaders and friends.

1986 - State Champions
First row, from left to right: Lavette Harris, Dawn Kolkman, Zanzy Moore, Anita Mendez, Trudi McCloud, Trina Merriweather, Kiwanna Johnson, Alisha Blash. Second row: Alice Belchner, Gloria Peoples, Jenny Osterman, Rhonda Lewis, Tahisha Bates, Barb Hooper, Tiffany McBride, Cori Kelso. Third row: DeeDee Nathan, Delana Neal, Kate Johnson, Tyjuana King, coach Walker, coach Stewart and coach Roberta Widmann-Foust.
photo by Watters

CHAPTER EIGHT
1990 - 1997
A. Jennifer Manth and South Side Pride

In January of 1990, principal Jack Weicker called a meeting of persons interested in forming an alumni association for South Side High School. Various informal alumni associations had existed at South Side as far back as the 1920's. These early alumni associations were primarily social in nature. It was Mr. Weicker's vision that this modern alumni association should have a formalized structure. It should also be organized according to applicable tax codes so that members could make financial contributions to aid South Side High School, and be able to deduct these sums on their tax returns. As a result of organizational meetings held in January and February of 1990, the South Side Alumni Association, Inc., was officially incorporated in April of 1990 and G. Stanley Hood was elected as first president. In order to establish an immediate treasury, life memberships were made available for a contribution of $1,000. During phase one of the life membership campaign, several individuals purchased these memberships. This enabled the alumni association to buy a computer. During the autumn of 1990 through the leadership of board members Barbara Miser Manges, Linda Vanderford Morris and Joy Wilkens Torrie lists of graduates from 68 classes were assembled and a permanent alumni office was established at South Side High School. Kathryn Zaegel, a graduate of the class of 1942, was hired as alumni secretary and manager of the permanent office. An alumni association newsletter entitled, "*Archer Arrows*" was established through the talented efforts and hard work of alumni association board members Bob Parker, Lois Bender Dinkel, Nancy Keller Mack and Lane Grile Ross.

In 1994, the South Side High School Foundation was established through the efforts of alumni association board member Paul Deal. The Foundation serves as a vehicle through which individuals can make South Side High School a part of their estate plan by making gifts and bequests. Under the leadership of alumni association board members Judith Robinson VanFossen and Janet Holtmeyer Weber, numerous scholarships have been awarded to graduating seniors. By 1995, the South Side High School Alumni Association, Inc., had given more than $50,000 to South Side High School and its students, and the South Side High School Foundation held investments worth more than $25,000. Examples of alumni association assistance to South Side High School are more than 20 $1,000 scholarships to graduating seniors, various forms of financial assistance rendered to students and clubs to attend out-of-town conferences, financial contributions to various clubs and to the media center, contributions to the Pride Corps for the purchase of uniforms, contributions for basketball team sweaters and gym bags for cheerleaders. Beginning with an appearance by alumni association president G. Stanley Hood at the 1991 South Side graduation ceremonies, the association has been a part of all South Side graduations bestowing complimentary one-year memberships on all members of the graduating class. Presidents of the alumni association since the initial organization have been Neil A. Anderson, Barbara Miser Manges, Lane Grile Ross, Carol Kettler Sharp and Darrell Blanton.

1991 – Jennifer Manth

In the spring of 1990, South Side students continued to gain distinction for themselves and their school and traditional Archer events of previous decades were still being observed. Matt Holly, a South Side junior, won an all-expense paid trip to Italy. Matt, a six-year newspaper carrier for the *Journal Gazette*, competed with other paper carriers in the Fort Wayne area for the trip which was sponsored by *Parade Magazine* in conjunction with the *Fort Wayne Newspapers*. In May of 1990, the annual Junior-Senior Prom was held at the Botanical Gardens, and the theme was "Here and Now." Later in the month of May, Dan Fulkerson crowned Denise Gerbers as Ivy Day Queen as this South Side tradition entered its seventh decade. Members of the 1990 Ivy Day court were Kristy Clark, Erin Fecher, Stacy Mims, Thao Ngo, Molly Walburn and Stephanie Wattley. The 1990 senior class play was "Get Smart." Detective Smart was portrayed by John Kimble while his sidekick, Agent 99, was played by Anita Fisher.[1]

The outstanding event occurring in the spring of 1990 was the decision of Jack Weicker to retire after serving 27 years as principal. Mr. Weicker's total length of service at South Side was 39 years. In a gigantic retirement dinner and testimonial held at the Scottish Rite Auditorium in June of 1990, hundreds of friends and colleagues, including former superintendent of schools Lester Grile and retiring superintendent Bill Anthis gathered to pay tribute to Mr. Weicker. Joining Jack Weicker in retirement in June of 1990 were assistant principal Richard Block who had completed 31 years of service at South Side, Robert Kelly, Dean and long-time speech coach completing 29 years of service, and long tenured teachers Robert Gernand (36 years), Richard Bussard (34 years), and James Tarr (27 years). The combined years of service of all of these retirees at South Side, including Mr. Weicker, was an astonishing 196 years![2]

Jack Weicker's choice to succeed him as principal was Jennifer Manth, a 1962 graduate of South Side High School. Jennifer Manth was approved by the school board and became principal of South Side in 1990. She was uniquely qualified to be principal due to her intimate knowledge of South Side customs

Celebrating as they have done three times before in the '80's, coach Bobbie Widmann-Foust and her 1989 state-champion track team show their enthusiasm for the crowd and the cameras.

photo by *The News-Sentinel*

Former principal Mr. Jack Weicker happily welcomes his new replacement
Miss Jennifer Manth as she enters the retirement party held in Mr. Weicker's honor.
photo by Watters

and traditions and her job experience within the Fort Wayne Community Schools. As a student at South Side, she graduated in the upper two percent of her class and was a member of the four-year honor roll and the National Honor Society. She won numerous awards while a student at South Side, including the prestigious Rowena Harvey Journalism Trophy. Following her graduation from South Side, she was admitted with distinction to Miami University in Oxford, Ohio where she graduated as a member of the Dean's Honor List, as well as serving as co-editor of the university yearbook. Ms. Manth has received two masters degrees, one in secondary education and a second degree in guidance, administration and supervision. Ms. Manth joined the Fort Wayne Community Schools in 1966 serving initially on special assignment in the Information Services Section where she published various newsletters, pamphlets, a junior high literary magazine and supervised journalism programs for the school system. In the late 1960's, she joined the faculty at Kekionga Junior High School as an English teacher where she taught for six years before going to Elmhurst High School. She first joined the South Side faculty in 1977 and served as head of the English Department before becoming a guidance counselor in 1979. From 1985 to 1987, she worked closely with her predecessor Jack Weicker while she served as assistant principal at South Side. From 1987 until her appointment as South Side principal in 1990, Jennifer Manth served as assistant principal at Northrop High School.[3]

As South Side High School opened in the autumn of 1990 under new principal Jennifer Manth, there were several challenges. The school was facing a declining enrollment, and there was still talk that South Side might be closed or in some way drastically changed. The South Side building, parts of which had not been renovated since the school opened in 1922, was in a state of decline and was deteriorating. Perhaps the greatest challenge was to convince a new superintendent that South Side High School could fulfill a unique function in the community and should continue to exist. Thanks to the leadership of Jennifer Manth, and a dedicated staff of administrators and teachers, coupled with the excellent foundation established by Jack Weicker, these challenges were met during the decade of the 90's. Skillfully organizing the assistance of parents, students, alumni, community leaders and friends, Jennifer Manth was able to rejuvenate the concept of South Side pride and not only lead the school into a new era, but to also mold the educational mission of South Side to continue to admirably serve the needs of its students.

In 1990, veteran South Side teacher Juanita Mendenhall was named FWCS Teacher of the Year. In November of 1990, director Sue Nelson and a group of talented actors and actresses brought "West Side Story" to the stage of the South Side auditorium. The lead roles were played by Dan Reeder and Lori David. In December of 1990, the annual "Spirit Week" was climaxed with the crowning of Elgin Reese as Homecoming King and Melissa Hollingsworth as Homecoming Queen.[4] On the sports scene, the girls' tennis team and the boys' varsity football team once again rose to prominence. The 1990 girls' tennis team was blessed with the presence of two of the most outstanding performers in South Side history, namely Kristy Clark and freshman Sarah Wagoner. Kristy Clark won 14 matches without a defeat in 1990. She had accomplished a 14-0 record in 1989.

FWCS Teacher of the year, Mrs. Juanita Mendenhall, graciously agrees to yet another interview by Channel 21 at the reception held in her honor.

photo by Jaboori

Freshman Sarah Wagoner also won 14 matches without a defeat in 1990 as the girls' tennis team reigned as co-champions of the SAC. Sarah Wagoner would also compile undefeated seasons in 1991, 1992, and finally in 1993 would lose one match. Sarah Wagoner's unbelievable four-year record at South Side is 64 victories and 1 defeat.[5] The 1990 Archer football team under coach John Hester won seven games and captured South Side's first and thus far only sectional title. Elgin Reese was named, "Most Valuable Player" of this team. Other outstanding performers included Joe Walburn, Ronnie Fowlkes, Joey Gold, Keith Hinton, Tony Brower, Thomas Blackburn, Corey Williams and Jermaine Leshore, who set a school record by scoring 16 touchdowns. In wrestling, Kancey Street went to the state finals, and the 1990-91 basketball team under coach Terry Flynn won 15 games and captured South Side's first sectional title in 11 years. Early in 1991, South Side defeated Angola to win its 1,000th basketball game in school history. This highly successful 1990-91 basketball team was led by senior Corey Williams who average almost 20 points per game. Underclassmen on this team included Joe Walburn and

Homecoming King Elgin Reese and Queen Melissa Hollingsworth.

Ryan Bond, talented sophomores who would become future Archer basketball stars.[6] In the spring of 1991, South Side had a swim team for the first time. It consisted of five freshmen, namely Heather Cassady, Nicole Close, Wendy Furphy, Sarah Melton and Christine Shank. The team was coached by Bill Close. In the sectional meet, Nicole Close received first place in the butterfly and the breast stroke and went on to compete at the state meet. In the Academic Super Bowl held at Indianapolis on April 27, 1991, the English squad consisting of juniors Dan Manco, Paul Naselaris and sophomore Steve Mullen took first place garnering not only the highest score in their division but the highest score of any division.[7]

At the recognition day ceremonies in May of 1991, a group of former South Side athletes known as the "South Side Has Beens" established a memorial for their former football and track coach Lundy Welborn, who had passed away in 1990. The "Lundy Welborn Most Valuable Athlete Award" was established at South Side. This award is given to the most valuable athlete in each sport. The members of the "Has Beens" committee presenting this award were George Hood, Bob Parker and Bob Berry. George Hood, captain of the 1929 Archer football team, made the presentation at the recognition assembly.[8] In June of 1991, at Memorial Coliseum, the annual South Side graduation ceremony was held. This was the first commencement ceremony presided over by Jennifer Manth. At the graduation ceremony, presentations were made by valedictorian Matt Holly, salutatorian Yahya Jaboori and superintendent of schools Williams Coats. At the end of her first year, principal Jennifer Manth could look back with much satisfaction. She had assembled an excellent administrative staff which included William Hedges and Frances Gooden as assistant principals and Eric Augsburger, a graduate of the South Side class of 1967, as assistant to the principal.[9]

As Archer students returned to school in the late summer of 1991, the dominant national headline was the surprising end of the Soviet Union. This significant national event followed the successful conclusion of the Persian Gulf War which took place early in 1991. On October 11, 1991, South Side hosted its first home varsity football game since the old stadium was abandoned following the 1970 sea-

"I did it!" exclaims graduate Stacy Mims, sharing her emotion with a friend.

photo by Watters

son. Since South Side was playing all of its home games at Wayne stadium and had been for 21 years, principal Jennifer Manth felt it would enhance school spirit to bring one home football game each season to the old South Side stadium.[10] The 1991 football team under coach John Hester posted its second consecutive winning season but was defeated in the first game of the sectional. Mike Woods was named to the First Team All SAC squad.[11]

The South Side Music Department's fall production in 1991 was "You're a Good Man Charlie Brown" while the Alpha Omega Club continued its history of sold out performances in December when it presented, "Showdown '91." The club showed its generosity and concern by donating 40 per cent of the "Showdown" profits to the sister of a South Side senior who was facing impending surgery. The M.C.'s of the "Showdown" were Senior Alpha Omega members Mike Woods, Cozette Church and Chris Pulliam. In January of 1992, the South Side Drama Club staged its production of "Fame." The leading roles were portrayed by Lori David and Tyrone Jackson. The Senior Banquet long a tradition at South Side was held in the Hamilton Room of the downtown Hilton Hotel on Sunday, February 16, 1992.[12] As the school year ended in the spring of 1992, students and faculty reflected upon the introduction of a completely new mathematics program at South Side. This new course of study was designed to cater to the learning ability of the individual student rather than gearing the presentation to the class as a whole. It allowed a student to advance in his or her math class at a comfortable and more natural rate. This innovative program was instituted by long-time Math Department head Richard Sage. At the recognition ceremonies in May of 1992, Erin Holly received the Wayne Scott Blanket for lettering in three sports for three years. Dan Manco became the first person in school history to have his name placed on all seven of the science trophies. In the same month, success for the South Side academic teams continued as the social studies academic team placed first at the Academic Super Bowl state competition in Indianapolis. Members of the winning team were Melissa Barcalow, Michael Garza, Steve Mullen, Janet Lubomirski and Chan Chantaphone. The coach of the state championship team was Mrs. Renee Albright.

As the 1992-93 school year began, principal Jennifer Manth declared it a "renaissance year" for South Side. The intent of the renaissance program was to get students involved in activities and show them that all school activities relate in some form. Each month, different subject areas were presented in a different format to the student body.[13] What the students and faculty could not possibly know as school opened in the fall of 1992 was that the year 1993 would indeed be the beginning of the "rebirth" of South Side High School. Veteran faculty members still teaching at South Side as the 1992-93 school year opened included George Robert Davis who had joined the faculty in 1957, Richard Sage who had first come to South Side in 1958, and athletic director Pres Brown who had first joined the staff in 1959. Additional long-time faculty members included Daniel Boylan, Neal Thomas, Allen Poorman, Kenneth Hullinger and Richard Melton, all of whom had joined the faculty in the 1960's. Among the new teachers were Kathleen Neuhaus, Grady Pruitt and Jenny Sanders.[14] Homecoming was moved to October instead of the normal mid-December time as Patrick Wilson and Markeishia Patterson were crowned king and queen respectively. The football team delighted the homecoming fans with an overtime victory. The 1992 Archer football team did not have an outstanding season but one of the outstanding individual performers in South Side football history closed out his high school career. During the 1990, 1991 and 1992 football seasons, quarterback Joe Walburn had rewritten the school record books by setting all-time career marks in complete passing yards, percentage of completed passes and total completed passes. In three seasons, Joe Walburn completed an amazing 321 passes.[15]

In November of 1992 under the direction of Sue Nelson, the South Side Music Department staged one of the most spectacular and ambitious programs in school history when the "Wizard of Oz" was presented. The unique feature of this production was the unusual number of cast members which totalled more than 300 students. Approximately 250 of these were South Side Spectrum elementary and middle school students who played munchkins, soldiers of the Emerald City, and members of the Oz court. Sue Nelson auditioned approximately 500 of these students before accepting 250 of them ranging from kindergarten through the eighth grade.[16] Among the outstanding events during the extremely eventful 1992-93 school year was the performance of the South Side boys varsity basketball team coached by Terry Flynn. This team, one of the greatest in Archer history, won 25 games during the regular season and tournament, which equals the victories produced by the superb South Side teams of 1938-39 and 1939-40. These 25 victories by an Archer basketball team have been exceeded only by the 1938 state championship team

The ratio of girls to guys at the 1989 M.O.R.P. was very much infavor of the guys as '89 seniors Dawn Buggs and Amy Olsen demonstrate with their newly found friend.

photo by Dunahue

'89 senior Don Manco congratulates '89 senior Thuy Ngo with a peck on the cheek as he crowns her 1989 Ivy Day Queen.

photo by Watters

Lead secretary Beverly Wyss takes a short break from the IBM "beast" to smile for the camera.   photo by Laslie

Mr. Paul Sidell, who taught at South from 1928 until 1965, shares his experiences with a metals shop class on V.I.P. Day. Mr. James Tarr welcomes the former South Side math department chairman with enthusiasm.   photo by Dunahue

which won 29 games and the 1958 state championship team which won 28 games.[17] The 1992-93 team won its first game of the season and then lost its second game to Huntington by one point. They then clicked off 19 consecutive regular season victories culminating with a one point victory over state ranked East Noble. They won three games in the sectional making it 22 victories in a row and then won two games in the regional to reach 24 consecutive wins before they lost to South Bend St. Joseph in the semi-state. The members of this amazing basketball team were Chris Dial, Jason Flynn, Ryan Bond, Joe Walburn, Josh Feay, Tyronne Walker, Scott Smiley, Cass Kruckeberg, Joe Miller, Kendall Chrismon and Robert Kizer. Senior Ryan Bond became the fourth Archer basketball player to score more than 1,000 career points.[18] Bond was named as a member of the Indiana High School All Star Team, the first South Side player so honored since Willie Long in the late 1960's.[19] A young sophomore on this team, Robert Kizer, would become South Side's fifth player to score more than 1,000 career points.

B. Renovation and the New Campus

In February of 1993, an architectural firm presented to the school board a feasibility study concerning the possible renovation of South Side High School. The architects determined that for 35.5 million dollars, South Side High School could become a state of the art facility comparable to the best high school buildings in the country. It was estimated that it would cost considerably more to close the existing South Side building and build a comparable school on another site. The study included the cost of buying 31 homes on approximately five acres of land northeast of the existing South Side building, relocating the football field to the north side of the new property and building bleachers, tennis courts and a

parking lot. For an additional 3.9 million dollars, the board could build a skating rink/swimming pool complex in a portion of the parking lot. The proposed renovation would add about 55,000 square feet of classrooms and building space to South Side High School. In addition, most of the South Side classrooms would have to be enlarged to comply with current state regulations. Superintendent William Coats told the board it would physically possible to close South Side and redistribute the 1,186 students to the district's other five high schools without overcrowding. However, he added he would strongly oppose any move too close South Side. Superintendent Coats told the board that South Side High School was an anchor in the community and should play a central role in the revitalization of the south side.[20]

This architectural feasibility study was the first major step in what would eventually become a 39.5 million dollar construction and renovation project which would completely transform South Side High School. For the next 12 months, the construction and renovation project was the subject of several school board meetings, public hearings, and state agency proceedings. As inevitably happens, there was some tax payer opposition to this large expenditure of public funds but in the final analysis, the school board and all necessary state agencies approved the project. By February of 1994, the massive South Side construction and renovation project was a reality.

As these board meetings, public hearings, and other legal proceedings connected with the renovation and construction project took place, life progressed normally at South Side High School. The 1993 prom entitled, "Midnight Memories" was held at the Botanical Gardens.[21] The week of April 23-30, 1993,

marked "Renaissance Culmination Week" where Archers were able to experience a parade and display different types of renaissance activities. South Side Spanish student Melissa Barcalow was the 1993 recipient of the Midland Modern Foreign Language Award. In addition, Latin teacher Judith Hahn was the 1993 recipient of the Classical Association of the Middle West and South Good Teacher Award. Hahn accepted the award at the annual meeting held at the University of Iowa in Iowa City on April 15-17, 1993.[22] Additional honors came to the South Side faculty when science teacher Francis Mustapha was not only selected as Fort Wayne Community Schools Teacher of the Year, but he also went on to capture the title of Indiana Teacher of the Year. [23] In May of 1993, South Side continued its long tradition of Ivy Day when Ryan Dunahue crowned Sara Kabisch as Ivy Day Queen. The 1993 Ivy Day court consisted of Melissa Barcalow, Sarah Wagoner, Kytela Green, Tiara Dixon, Markeishia Patterson and Vaudreca Lee.[24] In June of 1993 veteran teachers Ronald Miller and Daniel Boylen retired.

Francis Mustapha

In the autumn of 1993, "Spirit Week" kicked off with a traditional Monday "Pajama Day," Tuesday was "Hat Day," Wednesday was "Backwards Day," Thursday was "Hippy Day," and Friday was, as always, "Green and White Day." In honor of homecoming, one of South Side's home football games which were still being played at Wayne Stadium was moved to the old South Side Stadium. October 15, 1993, was the homecoming game, and it was the last game ever to be played in the old South Side Stadium. Philo won the homecoming banner contest and a prize of $15. Kareem Howell and Christina Yoder were crowned Homecoming King and Queen respectively. In the autumn of 1993, South Side's junior class (the class of 1995) elected all female officers. They chose Lindsay Miller as president, Kate Holly as vice president, Nakia Barnett as secretary, and Sara Melton as treasurer. Becky Dietle, Sarah Becker and Sara Glasgow were elected to the Social Committee.[25] Also in the autumn of 1993, Sarah Becker became South Side's first winner of the girls SAC cross country championship.[26] On January 15, 1994, the successful "Showdown Talent Show" put on by the Alpha Omega Club played to a sell-out audience for the fourth consecutive year.[27]

Following the completion of the highly successful 1992-93 basketball season, Archer coach Terry Flynn stepped aside turning the reigns over to South Side graduate and former varsity player Greg Taylor. The 1993-94 Archer basketball squad had its ups and downs winning 13 games and losing in the first game of the sectional. This team was led by junior Robert Kizer who averaged nearly 20 points per game. Even though this team did not achieve a high level of success, they were to participate in one of the outstanding moments in South Side Archer athletic history. On Friday night, February 4, 1994, the Archer basketball team was to face the state ranked Northrop Bruins in the final varsity basketball game at the South Side gym. By this

Francis Mustapha - Indiana Teacher of the Year.

time, the construction and renovation project was a reality and the 72-year old gymnasium was to be demolished so that a magnificent new media center could be constructed in its place. Before a "standing room only" crowd, the surprising Archers took an early lead over the favored Bruins. By the end of the third quarter, Northrop had tied the score and they took a five-point lead in the fourth quarter. South Side then closed the gap and with seconds remaining, the score was tied 54-54. At this point, the Archers took a time out and diagramed a special play for Robert Kizer. Kizer took the inbound pass in the back court, worked his way up the left side and as time expired fired a long shot which went in giving South Side a dramatic 56-54 victory. The Archer fans poured onto the floor knowing that this would be their final opportunity to savor a victorious moment in their beloved South Side gym. Archer basketball history had completed a full cycle from that opening game in December of 1922 when Alan "Red" Fromuth had scored the first South Side field goal in the new gymnasium leading the Archers to that memorable 8-7 victory over Shortridge to Robert Kizer's final dramatic field goal on February 4, 1994.[28] The final basketball game in the old gym was actually an alumni game played several days after the South Side-Northrop contest. Within hours after the conclusion of this alumni basketball game, workmen descended upon the old gymnasium and started to dismantle it.

In the spring of 1994 as the school year neared its end, the prom was moved to the Chamber of Commerce after many years at the Botanical Gardens. Lanita Benson was crowned as 1994 Ivy Day Queen. The prom was not the only South Side event which changed locations. In 1994, graduation was moved to the Scottish Rite Auditorium after many years at the Coliseum.[29] Retiring in June of 1994 were longtime faculty veterans Richard Sage and Pres Brown. Mr. Sage who joined the South Side faculty in 1958 was the long-time head of the Math Department succeeding Paul Sidell in the mid-1960's. Mr. Brown who had joined the South Side faculty in 1959 will be best remembered as the highly successful athletic director. He held this position for 21 years. He assumed the position of athletic director following the retirement of Wayne Scott in 1973. Mr. Brown rendered a tremendous service to South Side High School by compiling all of the athletic records at the time of the 50th anniversary in 1972. Many of these records came from the official score books kept by Ora Davis and R. Nelson Snider. With the retirements of Richard Sage and Pres Brown, South Side's final link with the 1950's was George Robert Davis, still a member of the faculty. Mr. Davis began his teaching career at South Side in the fall of 1957.

As students left the building in June of 1994, they were replaced by construction workers. The

1992-93 Varsity Basketball:
Row 1 - Chris Dial, Jason Flyn, Ryan Bond, Joe Walburn, Josh Feay, Tyronne Walker.
Row 2 - Coach Terry Flynn, Scott Smiley, Cass Kruckeberg, Joe Miller, Kendall Chrismon, Robert Kizer, Coach Greg Taylor

Ryan Bond

ground breaking ceremony for the South Side High School renovation took place on June 7, 1994. The ceremony was an outdoor affair taking place on the still vacant area where Archer Field now stands. Included in the impressive ceremony were remarks by school board president Leslye Mohrman, interim superintendent James Easton, Mayor Paul Helmke and principal Jennifer Manth. The senior class officers presented commemorative ivy and the board of school trustees presented a tablet officially designating the olympic sized swimming facility as the "Helen P. Brown Natatorium." Helen P. Brown, former president of the school board had been a long-time South Side advocate and was instrumental in the creation of the building and renovation project. She passed away shortly before the ground breaking ceremony.

As school opened in the late summer of 1994, the scene was reminiscent of that which had unfolded when the doors of South Side first opened in the autumn of 1922. Students and staff were crowded into one section of the building while an army of construction workers took over the rest of the facility to begin working their renovation magic. Among the first things to change were the long-standing ramps which were torn out and replaced by stairs. The only ramps to remain would be those immediately inside the north entrance of the building which were adjacent to the new media center, the site of the former gymnasium. In addition, the student locker rooms disappeared replaced by lockers in rows on the walls scattered throughout the building. This was to save space and create less traffic. During the 1994-95 and 1995-96 school years, the renovation project dominated practically all areas of school life. The renovation was to consist of three different phases. The first phase was renovation of a major portion of the academic wing located in the north half of the building. This phase

Naylon Thomson planting ivy.

also included construction of the Helen P. Brown Natatorium, the football stadium, the gymnasium, the parking lot and the removal of asbestos. Phase one was scheduled to be completed in September of 1995. Phase two involved renovating the south academic wing with a scheduled completion date of January, 1996 while phase three included renovations in the auditorium, cafeteria and music area scheduled for completion when school opened in the late summer of 1996.

Because of the construction of a new football stadium, Clinton Court was vacated between Darrow and Packard Avenues. All of the homes that were once located on the east side of Clinton Court between Darrow and Packard were purchased by the Fort Wayne Community Schools and were demolished. The site of the old football stadium became a parking lot. The Helen P. Brown Natatorium (olympic-size swimming facility) was constructed at what used to be the north end of the old stadium abutting Packard Avenue. The old gymnasium was replaced by a magnificent media center while a brand new gymnasium was constructed on the far east side of the campus abutting Clinton Street. As a result of construction and renovation the new South Side campus extends from Oakdale on the south to Packard on the north and from Calhoun on the west to Clinton on the east.[30]

In the late summer of 1994, Mike McMillen joined the faculty as athletic director replacing Pres Brown. In addition, Roberta Widmann-Foust, architect of South Side's magnificent girls track program in the 1980's returned after a two-year absence at Elmhurst. She would be serving as assistant to the principal. The freshmen class in the autumn of 1994, numbered 387 which was the laraest freshmen class in many years. Grady Pruitt replaced John Hester as head football coach. Mr. Hester retired from this position after coaching the Archer grid squads for 11 seasons. Archer football honors during the 1994 season went to senior lineman Drece Guy and junior defensive back Adrian Reese who were voted to the first team All SAC on defense. Guy was also voted to the All State team.

With the exception of news pertaining to renovation and construction, the most noteworthy event occurring at South Side High School in the autumn of 1994 was the announcement that South Side would soon become the second school in the state to offer the International Baccalaureate Diploma. Under the leadership of principal Jennifer Manth, South Side had first applied for the program in the fall of 1993. The application process included an on-site visit, a review of the teaching staff and a review of the school's curriculum. Students who chose to participate must begin the program during their junior year. By the time they graduate, they must pass exams in six areas of study, English, a foreign language, experimental science, individuals and society, mathematics, and an elective.[31] In offering the International Baccalaureate Diploma, South Side became one of approximately 100 schools in the nation to afford students the opportunity to pursue this unique course of study. Janet Perez, veteran South Side teacher, was named coordinator of South Side's International Baccalaureate program. During the 1994-95 school year, under the capable guidance of coach Marcia Rosene, South Side's speech program returned to the championship status it had enjoyed in previous years. Shonna Repine won first place at the State Congress Speaking Tournament.[32] On the club scene, the Section K basketball pep club was revived after an absence of several years. The boys soccer team, a relatively new organization at South Side, won the sectional title as Jamar Beasley set school records for most goals and most assists.[33]

On the basketball court, the girls varsity team coached by Don Shaidnagle lost in the final game of the sectional. Freshman Vnemina Reese led the SAC in scoring as well as being named to the first team All SAC.[34] The 1994-95 boys varsity basketball team, the second coached by Greg Taylor, had an outstanding season winning 23 games and losing only 3. This team won the sectional title but unfortunately lost to North Side in the regional. Robert Kizer and Cameron Stephens made first team All SAC and Robert Kizer became the fifth Archer player in history to score more than 1,000 career points. He joined former Archer greats Tom Bolyard, Willie Long, John Flowers and Ryan Bond in reaching 1,000 points. Junior Adrian Reese led the SAC in assists averaging over eight per game and set both the single season and career assist record at South Side with over 200 assists.[35] Robert Kizer and Joe Miller had the honor of being placed on the McDonald's All American Team.[36] In the spring of 1995, it was announced that South Side had received a 1995 Athletic Management Award of Excellence for its exemplary work in revitalizing the school's athletic facilities.[37] Also in the spring of 1995, girls' golf was introduced at South Side. South Side's first girls' golf team was made up of Jennifer Uslar, Amie Bishop, Leah GiaQuinta, Megan Pahmier and Carrie Uslar. In the spring of 1996, Jennifer Uslar set a school record for nine holes when she shot a 48 at Fairview Golf Course.[38] Senior Brandon Ridley ended an outstanding high school track career in the spring of 1995. He won the SAC, sectional and regional in the 400 meters four years in a row. During his senior year, he placed second at state.[39] After a one-year hiatus at the Chamber of Commerce, the Junior-Senior Prom returned to its usual place at the Botanical Conservatory in the spring of 1995. On May 26, 1995, South Side observed its 60th Ivy Day since the event was first celebrated in 1936. The 1995 Ivy Day Queen was Kate Holly, and the members of her court were Sarah Melton, Christie Hyser, Christine Shank, Kristen Woods and Tandeka Anderson. At Senior Recognition Day in May of 1995, each graduating student walked away with a special award, a hard hat just like the construction workers wore. In addition, a senior video was created under the direction of faculty members Phyllis Bush, chairman of the English Department, and Donna Roof. This video captured scenes from the senior classes' years at South Side. On June 9, 1995, South Side held its 73rd graduation ceremony at the Scottish Rite Auditorium. The top two scholastic places in the graduating class went to twins as Brent David Ringenberg was named valedictorian and Ryan Matthew Ringenberg was named salutatorian.[40] Retiring from the faculty in June of 1995 were long-time teachers Juanita Mendenhall and Richard Melton, as well as South Side graduate Neal Thomas. All of these teachers had originally joined the South Side faculty in the late 1960's.

Robert Kizer

"Pride and Participation" was announced by Jennifer Manth as the theme at the beginning of the 1995-96 school year. The enrollment of South Side was growing again as 1,342 students answered the opening bell. The freshmen class which numbered 514 was the largest in many years.[41] The 1995-96 school year was the second consecutive year to be dominated by the renovation and construction project. Many of the phase one projects had been completed and the students and staff were beginning to reap benefits from the chaos of construction. South Side's magnificent new football stadium named "Archer Field" opened on Friday evening, August 25, 1995, featuring a game with perennial state power Bishop Dwenger. Before a "standing room only" crowd, the Archer football team trailed by 21 points before scoring five consecutive touchdowns in an 18-minute period to stun the heavily favored Bishop Dwenger Saints with a 41-27 victory. This victory brought back memories of the 40-15 triumph over Central Catholic in South Side's last true home game in the old stadium in 1970. The first South Side touchdown scored in the new Archer Field was tallied by Adrian Reese on a five-yard run in the second quarter. The first South Side touchdown pass was from Adrian Reese to Tony Macon in the third quarter. The first kick off in Archer Field history was by Noah Sheray of the Archers. Byron Driver scored another Archer touchdown on a 14-yard pass from Adrian Reese. Adrian Reese continued to be prominent in the early history of Archer Field as he was crowned Homecoming King later in the 1995 season when homecoming was held for the first time in the new facility. Tameka Williams was crowned Homecoming Queen.[42]

In the autumn of 1995, South Side's show choir, "The Sound Waves" competed at various locations around the state, and Amanda Bokhart once again placed first in ISSMA state competitions. The Performing Arts Department staged an unusual two in one Shakespearean production as they performed "Kiss Me Kate" and "The Taming of the Shrew." Leading roles were taken by Desmond Crumpacker, Carolyn Furno, Emma Searle and Brian Porter. This production was directed by Sue Nelson. The last production to be held in the old auditorium before renovation was "Fame." The lead roles were filled by Lara Wheeler and Tamiko Pearson. Also in the autumn of 1995, the outstanding performer in girls' cross country was Evelyn Corona who set a home course record at Tillman Park and also set a new school record for the girls 3200 meter run. She was named to the Indiana All Star cross country team.[43] In October of 1995, another long-standing South Side tradition continued as Philo's Powder Puff football game was played.[44]

On Friday evening, December 1, 1995, another historic inaugural event in South Side High School athletic history took place as the new gymnasium named "Archer Arena" hosted its first boys varsity game. Unfortunately South Side lost to South Bend LaSalle by a score of 76-71. The honor of scoring South Side's first basket in the new gymnasium in a boys varsity game went to 6 foot 8 inch South Side center Cameron Stephens. As Stephens broke toward the basket from the left, guard Adrian Reese

So proud! Coach Walker and senior Evie Corona have been through a lot, but this year their work paid off.

photo by Hall

lobbed a pass to the front of the rim. Stephens grabbed it and dunked the ball. The Archers leading scorer in this game was Andy Smith with 18 points.[45] The 1995-96 girls basketball team coached by Don Shaidnagle won 11 games which was their best victory production in many seasons. Among the outstanding players were Bridget Shaidnagle, Jennifer Uslar, Vnemina Reese and Elise Hall. The boys varsity basketball team coached by Greg Taylor in his third year won more than 20 games for the second consecutive year, something that hadn't been accomplished since the 1977 and 1978 seasons. In addition, the boys team repeated as SAC champions and also captured their second straight sectional title. The team lost in the regional to Dwenger. In three seasons as head Archer basketball coach, Greg Taylor had two straight 20-game victory seasons.[46] The girls varsity volleyball team struggled to win but produced outstanding individual players such as Vnemina Reese, Lara Wheeler, Amber Colderbank and Jenny Ross who -made the All SAC second team as a sophomore. All SAC first team selections from the boys basketball team were Cameron Stephens, Adrian Reese and Omar Cooper.[47]

Early in 1996, the South Side Pride Corps went to Orlando, Florida to compete in the National Championship held at Disney World. During the previous summer, Cathy Lewis and Lara Wheeler had won individual awards for their dance ability. The captains of this outstanding Pride Corps were Angie Sherazi and Tamiko Pearson.[48] During the 1995-96 school year, the Academic Team had an outstanding year. Members of this team coached by Mrs. Renee Albright were Nicole Hoffman, Franco Holder, Thea Freygang, Todd Weber, Khalid Jaboori, Janelle Bailey, David Love, Ben Kellogg, Jason Tyler, Raul Rubalcada, Joe Lubomirski, Jenee Johnson and Carrie Klugman. 1996 also saw the end of the careers of three of the greatest individual wrestlers in South Side history. Bobby Green closed out his career with 57 wins, while Jason Ward finished his career with 76 wins and finished fifth at the state finals. Jerry Miller set a school record of 85 career victories including a record breaking 29 victories during the 1995-96 season. These outstanding wrestlers joined Rodney Bolden who had finished second at state in his weight division in 1992. The 1996 baseball team under coach Mark Redding won 13 games, the highest victory production in 12 years.

At 5:15 a.m., on Monday, April 8, 1996, a significant event in South Side renovation history took place. At that early morning hour, principal Jennifer Manth invited members of the school administration and the public to a "splash down" which formally opened the Helen P. Brown Natatorium. The master of ceremonies for the event was Bill Close, the natatorium manager and former gymnastics coach and swimming coach at South Side. The magnificent olympic-size swimming pool contains 612,000 gallons of water and the circulation system is able to circulate the water through the filtration system at the rate of 1,650 gallons per minute.

Friday, May 31, 1996, was a special day at South Side High School. This was the 60th anniversary of Ivy Day, one of South Side's most revered traditions. The usual Ivy Day events, including the parade, the planting of the ivy and the crowing of the queen and presentation of her court took place. Tameka Williams was chosen as Ivy Day Queen, and the members of her court were Elise Hall, Jill Stevenson, Glenda Perez, Emily Jackson, Amie Bishop and Michelle Lewis.[49] A special added feature of this Ivy Day was the naming of Jack Weicker as principal emeritus of South Side High School. Jack Weicker was a teacher and administrator at South Side for 39 years, including 27 years as principal. Accepting the unique honor as principal emeritus, he stated that he had many wonderful memories of South Side but what was always important to him were the students. He stated, "We taught kids from some of the wealthiest families in town, as well as some of the poorest kids in town, it was our job to make education viable for all those people and the staff worked hard to do it."[50] In June of 1996, South Side's 74th graduation took place at the Scottish Rite Auditorium. The valedictorian of the class of '96 was Dan Williams and the salutatorian was Elise Hall.[51]

In June of 1996, one of the most significant retirements in South Side High School history took place as George Robert Davis retired from the staff. Mr. Davis was head of the Science Department, taught chemistry, and was South Side's last link with the 1950's. George Robert Davis joined the South Side faculty in the autumn of 1957 and taught at the school for 39 years. He was the long-time sponsor of the Lettermen's Club and founded the Cinderellas who were a group of girls who helped out at track meets. Mr. Davis graduated from South Side in 1952 and was a member of the varsity track team. His father, Ora Davis, was a former South Side teacher, athletic director and guidance counselor who taught at the Archer school for 40 years.

First boys varsity game in new gymnasium. Junior Cameron Stephens thrills the crowd and leaves LaSalle opponents in awe with one of his famous dunks.
photo by Spicer

Here she is Miss America...
1995 Senior Kate Holly was elected Queen of the 1995 Ivy Day cremony. Kate and her court were elected by fellow seniors.

photo by Rutkowski

C. Diamond Jubilee

In the late summer of 1996, South Side High School opened its doors to students to begin its 75th year of service to the community. The enrollment continued to grow with almost 1,500 students present. Principal Jennifer Manth announced that the theme for the 1996-97 academic year would be "Pride and Performance." As the faculty returned for South Side's 75th year, among the new members were three South Side graduates, namely Joe Dietche, Donna Garringer and Kirby Volz, who were returning to teach at their alma mater as many before them had done.[52] These new faculty members will join veteran teachers still at South Side such as Allen Poorman and Kenneth Hullinger, both of whom started their South Side teaching careers in the late 1960's and Gary Black and Beverly Jones, who have been members of the faculty for more than 25 years.

Principal Jennifer Manth announced that the renovation and construction project was nearly complete. On November 2, 1996, South Side hosted a gigantic dedication and 75th anniversary celebration. The general chair person of the 75th anniversary celebration was G. Stanley Hood, while Jennifer Manth served as executive chair person. Meg Pahmier and Jean Johnson were in charge of publicity. The program chairmen were Charlene Holly and Dan Holly while awards and tours were handled by George Robert Davis and Linda Jackson. Julie Klugman and Donita Mudd were in charge of the reception committee. The master of ceremonies for the 75th anniversary and dedication celebration was Steve Shine, an Archer graduate.[53] Among the events included in the 75th anniversary and dedication celebration were the formal dedication of the Helen P. Brown Natatorium, dedication of the main building, tours of the campus and a reception, and a program entitled, "South Side Through the Decades" directed by Sue Nelson and presented in the newly renovated auditorium. In addition, South Side High School presented awards to approximately 60 distinguished alumni. Community dignitaries including Mayor Paul Helmke and Superintendent of Schools Dr. Thomas Fowler-Finn spoke at the event.

As this book goes to press, South Side High School, its students and teachers are still making news. The history of this great institution is literally a never-ending cycle. For example, South Side freshman Molly Sanders won the Summit Athletic Conference Varsity Girls Cross Country Meet.[54] The Archer football team under coach Grady Pruitt just completed its regular season with a resounding 39-6 victory over Elmhurst. In this game, Tony Macon and Luon Spearman were the top individual performers...and so it goes.

"South Side and its decorated history is a poignant symbol of American education and more profoundly it is a testament that the 'American melting pot' really works. It is at South Side where the ideal convictions of human equality are embraced and taught to students. It is at South Side where students learn the differences in racial or ethnic groups are results of environmental differences, not those of heredity. It is at South Side where students and teachers realize that America must utilize the potential of all its people to be a truly great nation. South Side truly is the epitome of the 'American melting pot.' South Side is an institution of education where Protestants and Catholics, Jews and Arabs, learn together regardless of their religious differences. South Side is a place where blacks and whites play football and basketball and wrestle together in healthy sport. South Side is a great monument of its community and symbolizes not only a school but a community solidly dedicated to making the United States a great nation by developing all human potential as fully as possible." This appropriate quote was written by South Side graduate Matt Holly and appeared in the 1990 *Totem*.

As we complete the final chapter in this book, the final chapter in the rich and varied history of South Side High School has not been written. As the baton is passed to a new generation of administrators, faculty and students and as this great institution marches forward into a new millennium and approaches its 100th anniversary, we are confident that it will continue to be what it has been for the past 75 years..."The school that has no equal."

Spirit is spelled S-O-U-T-H: Seniors Jennie Aiken, Evie Corona, Bridget Shaidnagle, Cassie Cress, Gina Lopez and Erika Spencer show their Archer spirit by spelling it out at the Swenger football game.

photo by Watters

CHAPTER ONE

1. *South Side Times*, 6 Oct., 1932
2. *Times*, 28 Dec., 1922
3. *Times*, 27 May, 1937
4. *Times*, 27 Apr., 1972
5. See Ward Gilbert Scrapbook (unpublished)
6. *Times*, 6 Oct., 1937
7. *Times*, 6 Oct., 1932
8. Parish, Robert, Interview by author, Ft. Wayne, IN, March 1995
9. *Times*, 8 Dec., 1922
10. *Times*, 27 Apr., 1972
11. Davis, George, Robert, Interview by author, Ft. Wayne, IN, April 1995
12. *Times*, 6 Oct., 1932
13. 1923 Totem
14. *Times*, 3 Nov., 1922
15. 1923 *Totem*
16. *Times*, 6 Oct., 1932
17. 1923 *Totem*
18. Ward Gilbert Scrapbook (unpublished)
19. "Indiana Grams" (newsletter of Sigma Alpha Epsilon Fraternity) Sept. 1958
20. *Times*, 28 Nov., 1922
21. *Times*, 15 Dec., 1922
22. Ward Gilbert Scrapbook (unpublished)
23. *Times*, 26 Jan., 1923
24. *Times*, 9 Mar., 1923
25. *Times*, 16 Mar., 1923
26. 1923 *Totem*
27. Ibid.
28. *Times*, 3 Nov., 1922
29. *Times*, 8 Dec., 1922
30. *Times*, 9 Feb., 1923
31. 1923 *Totem*
32. Ibid.
33. Ibid.
34. Ibid.
35. Ibid.
36. Ibid.
37. Ibid.
38. Ibid.
39. *News Sentinel*, 24 May, 1947 (Roto Section).
40. Ora Davis Memoirs (unpublished)
41. Hoffman, John, Interview with author, Ft. Wayne, IN, April 1995
42. 1924 and 1925 *Totems*
43. *Times*, 12 Oct., 1923
44. *Times*, 28 Sept., 1923
45. 1924 *Totem*
46. *Times*, 7 Dec., 1923
47. *Times*, 6 Oct., 1923
48. Davis, Sara, Interview by author, Ft. Wayne, IN, June 1995
49. 1924 *Totem*
50. *Times*, 11 Jan., 1924
51. McMillen, Mike, "South Side High School Athletic History, 1922-1996" (Unpublished)
52. *Times*, 20 Nov., 1924
53. *Times*, 10 Apr., 1925
54. 1925 *Totem*
55. *Times*, 15 Oct., 1925
56. *Times*, 5 Nov., 1925
57. 1926 *Totem*
58. Ibid.
59. *Times*, 19 Nov., 1926
60. *Times*, 4 Dec., 1925
61. *Times*, 25 Feb., 1926
62. *Times*, 18 Feb., 1926
63. *Times*, 31 May, 1963
64. Ibid.
65. *Times*, 8 Sept., 1926
66. *Times*, 31 May, 1963
67. Ora Davis memoirs (Unpublished)
68. 1927 *Totem*
69. Brown, Pres, "South Side Archers Athletic History 1922-1972"
70. 1927 *Totem*
71. Ibid.
72. Quarter Century Club listing
73. 1929 *Totem*
74. 1928 *Totem*
75. 1929 *Totem*
76. *Times*, 22 Nov., 1928
77. *Times*, 7 Dec., 1928
78. *Times*, 13 Dec., 1928
79. *Times*, 21 Mar., 1929
80. *Times*, 2 May, 1929
81. *Times*, 9 Sept., 1929
82. Ibid.
83. *Times*, 21 Nov., 1929
84. *Times*, 19 Dec., 1929

CHAPTER TWO

1. South Side *Times*, 13 Feb.,1930
2. *Times*, 6 Feb., 1930
3. *Times*, 20 Feb., 1930
4. *Times*, 11 Sep., 193
5. Parker, Bob, Interview with author, Ft. Wayne, IN, June 1995
6. 1931 *Totem*
7. *Times*, 31 May, 1963
8. 1931 Greenbook
9. *Times*, 9 Apr., 1931
10. 1932 *Totem*
11. Ibid.
12. 1933 *Totem*
13. 1934 *Totem*
14. 1933 *Totem*
15. Ibid.
16. *Times*, 6 Sep., 1933
17. 1934 *Totem*. The precise date that Jack Wainwright wrote the words of the South Side Alma Mater is unknown. The words of the alma mater appear for the first time in the September 11, 1936, issue of the South Side *Times*.
18. Ibid.
19. 1935 *Totem*
20. Ibid.
21. Ibid.
22. Bormuth, Ruth and Turflinger, Dorothy, "History of South Side High School" (unpublished)
23. *Times*, 19 Sep., 1935
24. *Times*, 27 Feb., 1936
25. *Times*, 20 Feb., 1936
26. *Times*, 14 May, 1936
27. *Times*, 7 May, 1936
28. *Times*, 14 May, 1936
29. 1936 *Totem*
30. Ibid.
31. 1937 *Totem*
32. Ibid.
33. Ibid.
34. Brown, Pres, "South Side Archers Athletic History, 1922-1972"
35. Tape recording of 1938 Muncie-South Side Super Regional game
36. Tape recording of 1938 state championship game
37. *Times*, 31 Mar., 1938
38. *Times*, 16 Mar., 1939
39. Brown, Op. cit.
40. *Times*, 31 Mar., 1938
41. *Times*, 29 Apr., 1937
42. *Times*, 28 Apr., 1938
43. *Times*, 27 Apr., 1939
44. *Times*, 30 Mar., 1939
45. *Times*, 1 Nov., 1937
46. *Times*, 11 Nov., 1937
47. *Times*, 7 Sep., 1938
48. *Times*, 21 Sep., 1938
49. *Times*, 20 Oct., 1938
50. *Times*, 6 Oct., 1938
51. *Times*, 12 Sep.,1939
52. *Times*, 12 Oct.,1939
53. *Times*, 28 Dec .,1939

CHAPTER THREE

1. South Side *Times*, 4 Jan., 1940
2. *Times*, 11 Jan., 1940
3. 1940 *Totem*
4. *Times*, 28 Mar., 1940
5. *Times*, 4 Apr., 1940
6. 1940 *Totem*
7. Brown, Pres, "South Side Archers Athletic History, 1922-1972"
8. *Times*, 9 May, 1940, and 1940 *Totem*
9. 1940 *Totem*
10. Ibid.
11. *Times*, 4 Apr., 1940
12. 1940 *Totem*
13. Ibid.
14. 1941 *Totem*
15. Brown, Op. cit.
16. 1941 *Totem*
17. Ibid.
18. Ibid.
19. Ibid.
20. Ibid.
21. 1942 *Totem*
22. *Times*, 4 Dec., 1941
23. *Times*, 27 Nov., 1941
24. *Times*, 5 Feb., 1942
25. 1942 *Totem*
26. Ibid.
27. "Twenty-Fifth Anniversary Program," 28 May, 1947. The one woman from South Side killed in World War II was Martha Webb, see *South Side Times*, 24 May, 1945.
28. *Times*, 13 Apr., 1944
29. *Times*, 31 May, 1963
30. Ibid.
31. Ibid.
32. Ibid.
33. *Times*, 18 Sep., 1942
34. *Times*, 31 May, 1963
35. Ibid.
36. Ibid.
37. Ibid.
38. VanGorder, Pauline, Interview with author, Ft. Wayne, IN March 1995
39. 1942 *Totem*
40. Ibid.
41. Ibid.
42. Ibid.
43. 1943, 1944, and 1945 *Totems*
44. 1944 *Totem*
45. 1943 *Totem*
46. Ibid.
47. 1944 *Totem*
48. 1945 *Totem*
49. 1944 *Totem*
50. 1945 *Totem*
51. 1944 and 1945 Totems
52. *Times*, 10 May, 1945
53. 1942 *Totem*
54. 1944 *Totem*
55. *Times*, 6 June, 1945
56. *Times*, 24 May, 1945
57. 1946 *Totem*
58. *Times*, 6 Dec., 1945
59. *Times*, 16 May, 1946
60. *Times*, 4 Sep., 1946
61. *Times*, 14 Nov., 1946
62. Brown, Op. cit.
63. 1945, 1946 and 1947 *Totems*
64. "Twenty-Fifth Anniversary Program," 28 May, 1947
65. Ibid.
66. Ibid.
67. 1947 *Totem*
68. Brown, Op. cit.
69. *Times*, 20 May, 1948
70. 1948 *Totem*
71. 1949 *Totem*
72. Ibid.
73. *Times*, 18 Mar., 1948
74. *Times*, 3 June, 1948
75. 1949 *Totem*
76. 1950 *Totem*
77. *Times*, 5 Jan., 1950

CHAPTER FOUR

1. *South Side Times*, 23 Jan., 1950
2. *Times*, 23 Feb., 1950
3. *Times*, 23 Mar., 1950
4. *Times*, 16 Mar., 1950
5. Sidell, Paul, Interview with author, Ft. Wayne, IN, July 1995
6. Davis, George, Robert, Interview with author, Ft. Wayne, IN, July 1995
7. 1950 *Totem*
8. 1951 *Totem*
9. 1952 *Totem*
10. 1953 *Totem*
11. Ibid.
12. 1950 *Totem*
13. 1951 *Totem*
14. Brown, Pres, "South Side Archers Athletic History, 1922-1972"
15. 1950, 1951 and 1952 Totems
16. 1952 *Totem*
17. Brown, Op. cit.
18. *Times*, 31 May, 1963
19. 1952 *Totem*
20. *Times*, 9 Oct., 1952
21. *Times*, 30 Oct., 1952
22. *Times*, 15 Jan., 1953
23. *Times*, 16 Apr., 1953
24. *Times*, 9 Sep., 1953
25. *Times*, 17 Sep., 1953
26. Ibid.
27. *Times*, 29 Oct., 1953
28. *Times*, 4 Mar., 1954
29. 1954 *Totem*
30. *Times*, 28 Apr., 1955
31. *Times*, 22 Sep., 1955
32. *Times*, 26 May, 1955
33. *Times*, 29 Sep., 1955
34. 1954 *Totem*
35. *Times*, 8 Sep., 1954
36. *Times*, 11 Nov., 1954
37. 1954 *Totem*
38. *Times*, 28 Oct., 1954
39. *Times*, 13 Jan., 1955

40. *Times*, 6 Jan., 1955
41. *Times*, 17 Mar., 1955
42. *Times*, 1 Dec., 1955
43. *Times*, 3 Nov., 1955
44. 1956 *Totem*
45. 1955 *Totem*
46. *Times*, 21 Apr., 1955
47. 1956 *Totem*
48. *Times*, 7 Sep., 1955
49. 1957 *Totem*
50. 1955 and 1956 *Totems*
51. 1957 *Totem*
52. 1956 *Totem*
53. 1954 *Totem*
54. 1955 *Totem*
55. 1956 *Totem*
56. 1955 *Totem*
57. Brown, Op. cit.
58. *Times*, 26 May, 1955
59. 1956 *Totem*
60. 1954, 1955 and 1956 *Totems*
61. 1956 *Totem*
62. 1957 *Totem*
63. Ibid.
64. Brown, Op. cit.
65. 1958 *Totem*
66. Brown, Op. cit.
67. 1957 *Totem*
68. Ibid.
69. Brown, Op. cit.
70. Ibid.
71. *Journal Gazette*, 23 Mar., 1958
72. *Indianapolis Times*, 23 Mar., 1958
73. 1958 *Totem*
74. *Times*, 31 May., 1963
75. 1958 *Totem*
76. Brown, Op. cit.
77. 1958 *Totem*
78. 1959 *Totem*
79. Ibid.
80. Ibid.
81. Brown, Op. cit.
82. 1959 *Totem*
83. Ibid .
84. Ibid.
85. 1960 *Totem*

CHAPTER FIVE

1. 1960 *Totem*
2. Ibid.
3. 1961 *Totem*
4. Ibid.
5. Ibid.
6. 1962 *Totem*
7. 1963 *Totem*
8. 1962 *Totem*
9. 1963 *Totem*
10. Weicker, Jack, Interview by author, Ft. Wayne, IN, June 1995
11. South Side *Times*, 31 May, 1963
12. Ibid.
13. *Times*, 27 Apr., 1972 (Fiftieth Anniversary Edition)
14. Luse, Mildred, Interview by author, Ft. Wayne, IN, June 1995
15. *Times*, 31 May, 1963
16. Sidell, Paul, Interview by author, Ft. Wayne, IN, July 1995
17. Graham, Mary, Interview by author, Ft. Wayne, IN Aug. 1995
18. Weicker, Interview
19. 1963 *Totem*
20. Weicker, Interview
21. 1964 *Totem*

22. Ibid
23. 1965 *Totem*
24. 1964 *Totem* and 1965 *Totem*
25. 1965 *Totem*
26. Ibid.
27. Ibid.
28. Ibid.
29. Ibid.
30. 1966 *Totem*
31. 1967 *Totem*
32. Ibid.
33. Ibid.
34. *Journal Gazette*, 15 Mar., 1967
35. 1966 *Totem*
36. 1967 *Totem*
37. Ibid.
38. 1966 *Totem*
39. 1968 *Totem*
40. 1967 *Totem*
41. 1966 *Totem*
42. Ibid.
43. 1967 *Totem*
44. Ibid.
45. 1968 *Totem*
46. 1967 *Totem*
47. 1966 *Totem*
48. Brown, Pres, "Outstanding Moments in South Side Athletics" (Unpublished)
49. Brown, Pres, "South Side High School Athletic History, 1922-1972." Two of South Side's state final appearances were in 1924 and 1929 when the finals were a 16-team affair.
50. Brown, Pres, "Oustanding Moments"
51. 1967 *Totem*
52. 1968 *Totem*
53. Brown, Pres, "Oustanding Moments"
54. Brown, Op. cit.
55. 1968 *Totem*
56. Ibid.
57. Ibid.
58. Ibid.
59. 1969 *Totem*
60. Ibid.
61. Ibid.
62. Ibid.
63. Ibid.
64. Ibid.
65. 1970 *Totem*

CHAPTER SIX

1. 1970 *Totem*
2. Ibid.
3. Ibid.
4. Ibid.
5. Brown, Pres, "South Side Archers Athletic History, 1922-1972"
6. 1970 *Totem*
7. Ibid.
8. Ibid.
9. 1971 *Totem*
10. Ibid.
11. Ibid.
12. South Side *Times*, 3 June, 1971
13. 1972 *Totem*
14. Ibid.
15. Ibid.
16. Ibid.
17. Ibid.
18. Brown, Op. cit.
19. 1973 *Totem*
20. McMillen, Mike, "South Side High School Athletic History,

1922-1996"
21. "Fiftieth Anniversary Program," 29,Apr., 1972
22. Ibid.
23. Weicker, Jack, "Comments at Fiftieth Anniversary Program," 29 Apr., 1972
24. 1973 *Totem*
25. Ibid.
26. Ibid.
27. Ibid.
28. Ibid.
29. Ibid.
30. Ibid.
31. Ibid.
32. McMillen, Op. cit.
33. 1974 *Totem*
34. McMillen, Op. cit.
35. 1974 *Totem*
36. Ibid.
37. Ibid.
38. Ibid.
39. Ibid.
40. 1975 *Totem*
41. Ibid.
42. Ibid.
43. Ibid.
44. Ibid.
45. 1976 *Totem* and 1977 *Totem*
46. 1976 *Totem*
47. 1975 *Tote*
48. Ibid.
49. Ibid.
50. Ibid.
51. Ibid.
52. Ibid.
53. 1975 *Totem*
54. Ibid.
55. Ibid.
56. 1976 *Totem*
57. Ibid.
58. McMillen, Op. cit.
59. 1976 *Totem*
60. 1977 *Totem*
61. McMillen, Op. cit.
62. 1976 *Totem*
63. 1977 *Totem*
64. McMillen, Op. cit.
65. 1977 *Totem*
66. Ibid.
67. 1976 *Totem*
68. Ibid.
69. 1977 *Totem*
70. 1978 *Totem*
71. 1979 *Totem*
72. Ibid.
73. 1977 *Totem*
74. 1978 *Totem*
75. Ibid.
76. 1979 *Totem*
77. McMillen, Op. cit.
78. Ibid.
79. 1979 *Totem*
80. Ibid.
81. McMillen, Op. cit.
82. Ibid.
83. 1980 *Totem*
84. Ibid.
85. Ibid.
86. Ibid.
87. Ibid.

CHAPTER SEVEN

1. 1980 *Totem*
2. 1981 *Totem*
3. Ibid.
4. Ibid.
5. Ibid.
6. Ibid.
7. 1982 *Totem*
8. 1980 *Totem*

9. 1981 *Totem*
10. 1983 *Totem*
11. 1981, 1982 and 1983 Totems
12. 1982 and 1983 Totems
13. Brown, Pres, "Outstanding Moments in South Side Athletics"
14. McMillen, Mike, "South Side High School Athletic History, 1922-1972"
15. 1981 *Totem*
16. Ibid.
17. McMillen, Op. cit.
18. 1982 *Totem*
19. Ibid.
20. 1983 *Totem*
21. Ibid.
22. McMillen, Op. cit.
23. 1984 *Totem*
24. Ibid.
25. Ibid.
26. Ibid.
27. Ibid.
28. Ibid.
29. Ibid.
30. 1983, 1984 and 1985 Totems
31. 1986 *Totem*
32. Ibid.
33. 1985 *Totem*
34. 1986 *Totem*
35. 1984 *Totem*
36. 1985 and 1986 Totems
37. 1985 *Totem*
38. Ibid.
39. 1986 *Totem*
40. Ibid.
41. 1984 and 1985 *Totems*
42. 1984 *Totem*
43. 1985 *Totem*
44. 1986 *Totem*
45. 1987 *Totem*
46. 1985 *Totem*
47. *Journal Gazette*, 20 Apr., 1986
48. 1987 *Totem*
49. Ibid.
50. Ibid.
51. Ibid.
52. Ibid.
53. 1988 *Totem*
54. 1987 *Totem*
55. 1988 *Totem*
56. Ibid.
57. 1989 *Totem*
58. 1989 and 1990 *Totems*
59. 1989 *Totem*
60. McMillen, Op. cit.
61. Ibid.
62. 1989 *Totem*
63. 1990 *Totem*
64. Ibid.
65. Frost Illustrated, 6-12 Dec., 1989
66. 1989 *Totem*
67. Frost Illustrated, 6-12 Dec., 1989

CHAPTER EIGHT

1. 1991 *Totem*
2. Ibid.
3. Manth, Jennifer, Interview by author, Ft. Wayne, IN, Oct. 1996
4. 1991 *Totem*
5. McMillen, Mike, "South Side High School Athletic History,1922-1996"
6. 1991 *Totem*
7. 1992 *Totem*
8. Ibid
9. 1991 *Totem*

10. 1992 *Totem*
11. Ibid.
12. Ibid.
13. 1993 *Totem*
14. Ibid.
15. McMillen, Op. cit.
16. *Journal Gazette*, 12 Nov., 1992
17. Brown, Pres, "South Side Archers Athletic History, 1922-1972"
18. 1993 *Totem*
19. McMillen, Op. cit.
20. *Journal Gazette*, 23 Feb., 1993
21. 1994 *Totem*
22. *South Side Times*, 7 May, 1993
23. 1994 *Totem*
24. Ibid.
25. Ibid.
26. McMillen, Op. cit.
27. 1994 *Totem*
28. *Journal Gazette*, 5 Feb., 1994
29. 1995 *Totem*
30. Ibid.
31. *Journal Gazette*, 11 Oct., 1994
32. 1995 *Totem*
33. McMillen, Op. cit.
34. 1995 *Totem*
35. Ibid.
36. McMillen, Op. cit.
37. *News Sentinel*, 1 Apr., 1995
38. McMillen, Op. cit.
39. 1996 *Totem*
40. Ibid.
41. "Archer Reports" Fall 1995
42. 1996 *Totem*
43. Ibid.
44. Ibid.
45. *Journal Gazette*, 2 Dec.,1995
46. 1996 *Totem*
47. *Journal Gazette*, 5 Mar.,1996
48. 1996 *Totem*
49. *Times*, 31 May, 1996
50. *News Sentinel*, 1 June, 1996
51. *Times*, 31 May, 1996
52. "Archer Reports" Fall 1996
53. *Times*, 31 May,1996
54. *News Sentinel*, 17 Oct ., 1996

INDEX

INDEX

G. Stanley Hood

G. Stanley Hood is a member of the South Side class of 1956. Following his graduation from South Side, he attended Indiana University where he received his undergraduate degree. He later received the Doctor of Jurisprudence Degree from the Indiana University School of Law. In 1990, Mr. Hood, a founding member, was elected first president of the South Side High School Alumni Association, Inc.

Mr. Hood is a partner in the law firm of Roby & Hood. He is the author of numerous historical and legal articles, and resides with his wife, Ruth, in Fort Wayne.